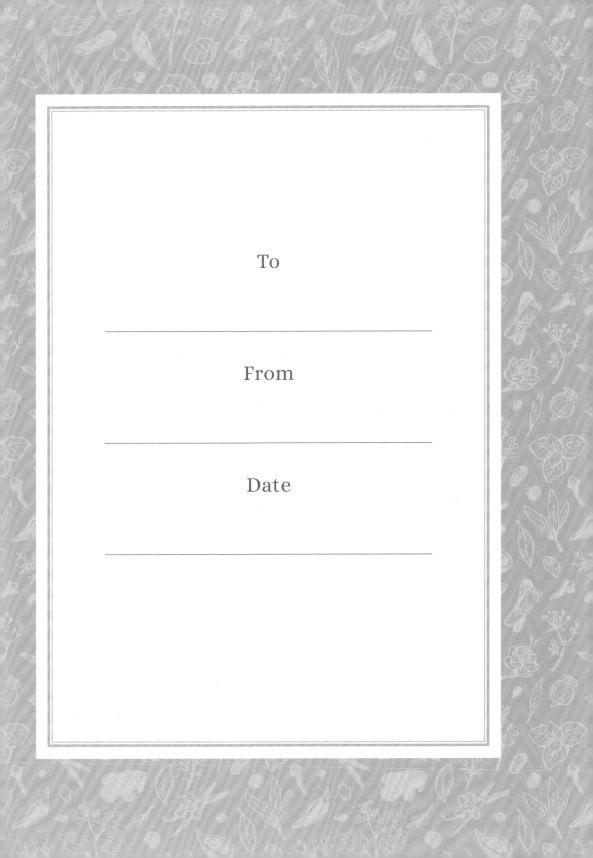

To

_____

From

_____

Date

_____

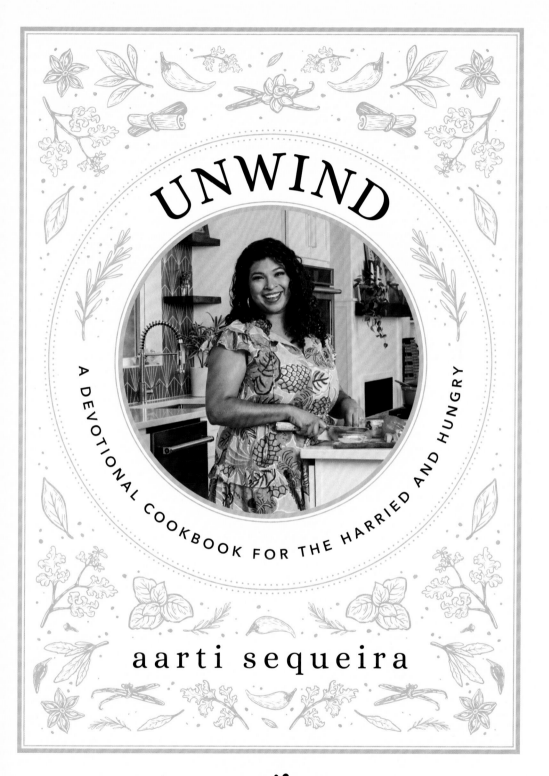

UNWIND

A DEVOTIONAL COOKBOOK FOR THE HARRIED AND HUNGRY

aarti sequeira

DaySpring
LIVE YOUR FAITH

Contents

Harried. Exhausted. Hungry.

Most days, this is me at about 4:30 p.m. Maybe you're familiar? It's that moment that feels like a finish line after a full day of work, responsibilities, conflict, and just, life. It "feels" like a finish line, but in reality, it's just a tease. The day isn't over. Nay, now I must muster up the remains of my strength and imagination to traverse the final hurdle: dinner.

"You?" I hear you cry. "You cook for a living! How can making dinner be hard for YOU?"

For some, cooking is an outlet, a time for jazz and a glass of wine, while a pot of pasta bubbles away merrily. I love that for them! But over the past few years, as the joy of cooking has become my daily grind too, it has begun to feel like salt in the wound for me, the final straw after a day of… so many straws. I look to one culinary guru after another, seeking simpler recipes, meal-prepping strategies, or one pot dinners.

But nothing sticks, and not only is my family left with the same plate of hot dogs, broccoli, and sweet potato tots that I pulled together the week before, but probably something worse: an Aarti with shoulders slumped over in defeat and sadness.

Then, I met Vibha.

> Now I must muster up the remains of my strength and imagination to traverse the final hurdle: dinner.

Vibha owns a popular Indian grocery-restaurant chain. I always addressed her as "Aunty" as Indian culture celebrates the fact that, in some ways, we're all family. One day, I peeked into her restaurant kitchen and noticed that none of her cooks were Indian, and yet her food was full of all the hallmarks of an authentic Indian meal.

"How did you manage that, Aunty?" I asked.

"Oh I've taught them everything," she said proudly, her kohl-rimmed eyes opening wide. "I even taught them to pray before they cook, just like I do."

Pray before you cook.

Those four words have changed the way I look at the kitchen entirely.

Instead of seeing it as yet another chore, the one keeping me from crossing the finish line straight into a piece of chocolate, a hot shower, and bed … I now see it as a threshold into the transcendent. Our kitchens are not torture chambers! They're temples in the making, a time and space to invite God to transform the mundane into the sacred.

What if, in the same way I take a deep breath when I walk into the sanctuary of a church, I allowed for a moment of stillness? Could I then see this preparation of the evening meal as a kind of evensong, that evening service of yore, when families everywhere would stop as the sun set to turn their eyes toward heaven and give thanks for a day of good and bad, hard and joyful, because in the end it's all good because it all came from the Father?

How would that change the way I looked at the evening meal?

How? Well, this book is how! I now see dinnertime as a time of connection—first with God and then with those around the table. In stopping at the threshold of the kitchen, I look for the thing I need in that moment: peace, courage, strength, reassurance … And wouldn't you know it? In asking for those things, God delivers. Sometimes it's an actual anointing of peace as I peel the layers of skin weighing down each clove of garlic. Sometimes it's a lesson about His timing, as I wait patiently on the onions to caramelize. Sometimes it's a lyric in the song I felt led to play on my phone. Folding my hands in prayer before I put my hand to the skillet opens my eyes to the truth that I'm not alone in the kitchen: His hands are on mine as I chop, His fingers are wiping away every tear, His strong shoulder steadies me as I falter.

> Folding my hands in prayer before I put my hand to the skillet opens my eyes to the truth that I'm not alone.

And so, these recipes aren't organized traditionally, by protein or type of dish. Instead, they center on how you might arrive at that threshold. Play some music that reminds you of the One who calls you *beloved*. Close your eyes and take a deep breath. What do you need right now? Hope? Comfort? To celebrate? Flip through the contents to find the word that most aligns with your heart. Each devotion focuses on one specific need, and how it's found in Jesus. Then, as you make the attached recipe, let those truths seep into every step of the process, nourishing you as you prepare something nourishing for the table. Or just do the devotional. Or just make the recipe! This book is for you. I had you in mind as I wrote every word, as I created every recipe. This book is to remind us that God is with us in every mundane moment, from the morning commute to the evening meal. In Him, every task is gilded in gold and pregnant with wisdom.

So come, cross the threshold with me, dear one. Come unwind from the day. Come be transformed from the harried and hungry … to the serene and satisfied.

Aarti

Scan for
additional content
from Aarti!

SECTION 01

When You Need a Fresh Start

CHAPTER 1

When You Need a Fresh Start

Have you ever gotten to a point where you're just totally and utterly sick of yourself? Whether it's my insecurities or my stubborn streak or the entire wreckage of neuron-firing synapses that make me the person I am, sometimes I fling myself at God, crying out, "Ugh, Lord! Why am I like this! Fix it, Jesus!"

The good news is that God is in the fresh-start business!

My daughters and I love watching videos of reptiles sloughing off their old, dried out skin to reveal the bright, shiny scales underneath. I've always wondered whether the poor creature is itchy or uncomfortable as the old is torn away.

> ## The good news is that God is in the fresh-start business!

> *"Therefore, if anyone is in Christ, he is a new creation. The old has passed away; behold, the new has come."*
> II CORINTHIANS 5:17 ESV

Perhaps when I'm craving a restart button, it's a sign that the old skin is ready to be sloughed off. The discomfort you're feeling right now is necessary, darling one, because it signals that the new creation is ready to be unveiled. Oh, what a delight! Rejoice in the discomfort because it means the new skin is about to be revealed in all its beauty and glory. In the Greek, the word old is *archaios*, which sounds an awful lot like archaic to me. The longing for a fresh start is a signal that the way you've operated thus far is outdated. It's not who you are anymore. It's time to leave it in the past.

Archaios also denotes a movement forward. As you walk toward where God is bidding, the old things may tug at you. The great preacher Charles Spurgeon once said that it was easier for God to create the world than to make new creations out of us, because the world never resisted His hand! But we have "our stubborn wills, our deep prejudices . . . all these, great God, opposed thee.[2]" Thank goodness that our Father is not only mightier than our will but also kind enough to overcome it for our benefit and His glory.

A fresh start is available to anyone in Christ, no matter who you are or what you've done. Reach out, sweet one. As you peel the papery skins off the tomatillos in this Salsa Verde Shakshuka, consider whether you have any old skins that need to come off. Offer them to God, and just you wait until you see the new one God has created specifically and uniquely for you.

A fresh start is available to anyone in Christ, no matter who you are or what you've done.

1"The Believer a New Creature," July 18, 1869, Metropolitan Tabernacle Pulpit, Vol. 15, https://www.spurgeon.org/resource-library/sermons/the-believer-a-new-creature/#flipbook/

Salsa Verde Shakshuka

MAKES 4 TO 6 SERVINGS | **TOTAL TIME:** 40 MINUTES | **ACTIVE TIME:** 20 MINUTES

Cook's Note: If you'd like to gussy this dish up, save the papery tomatillo husks and deep fry them! Season with lots of salt and serve them with the Shakshuka. They lend a happy herbal note to the dish.

½ pound tomatillos

1 poblano chili, halved lengthwise (membranes removed to control heat)

2 cloves garlic, unpeeled

1 jalapeño, seeds and membranes removed, roughly chopped

¼ cup cilantro leaves and soft stems, plus extra for garnish

1 tablespoon lime juice (about ½ a lime), plus 1 extra lime for serving

3 to 4 leeks, white and light green parts only, halved lengthwise and sliced into half moons (rinsed well)

½ cup chicken stock, plus extra as needed

¼ cup avocado oil or other neutral oil

4 to 6 large eggs

Cotija cheese

2 avocados, sliced for serving

Corn tortillas, warmed

1. Set oven rack 6 inches from broiler element and turn broiler on.

2. Remove papery husks from the tomatillos. Rinse tomatillos and slice in half. Lay tomatillos and poblano chili, cut side down, onto a foil-lined sheet pan, alongside the garlic cloves in their skin. Pop under the broiler for 7 to 9 minutes, until tomatillos soften and poblano skin browns slightly. Remove from the oven.

3. Place poblano chili halves in a bowl. Cover with plastic wrap, and set aside for 5 minutes.

4. Meanwhile, add avocado oil and leeks to a large skillet and set it over medium heat. Cook until they soften and turn translucent, 15 to 20 minutes.

5. Peel the skin off the poblano chili and garlic cloves, then toss into the blender along with tomatillos, jalapeño, cilantro, lime juice, and ½ cup chicken stock. Blend until smooth. Season with salt.

6. Pour this salsa verde over the softened leeks. Add additional stock, if needed, to make a sauce similar in consistency to a pasta sauce (about ¼ cup). Using the bottom of a ladle or flat-bottomed glass, create divots in the sauce for the eggs. Crack an egg into each divot and season them with salt. Turn heat down to low, cover and cook until eggs are to your liking, about 8 minutes for a runny yolk.

7. To serve, top with a good sprinkle of cotija cheese and fresh cilantro. Serve alongside warm corn tortillas, sliced avocado, and wedges of lime.

CHAPTER 2

When You Need a Reason to Rise and Shine

I will greatly rejoice in the LORD;
my soul shall exult in my God,
for he has clothed me with the garments of salvation;
he has covered me with the robe righteousness,
as a bridegroom decks himself like a priest with a beautiful headdress,
and as a bride adorns herself with her jewels.

ISAIAH 61:10 ESV

There was a period in my life when I'd open my eyes in the morning, stare at the ceiling, and whisper to God, "Why did You wake me up this morning? Why don't You just take me home? This life is too hard."

Sometimes it's hard to see any point in getting up. I get it. But this verse reminds us that we have the greatest reason in the world to jump out of bed, rejoicing. It's the opposite of the tale of "The Emperor's New Clothes." He sashayed around town, showing off an imaginary suit of velvet and lace, only to find that his near-nakedness was very much on display. We get to march through life in power and beauty, our nakedness replaced by the most resplendent robes ever seen on earth: the garments of salvation.

> Not only has He clothed you with such finery . . . but He also has a purpose for you.

It makes me think of the day when someone sent my two daughters, then wee toddlers, the dresses of their dreams: emblazoned with gold unicorns on the chest, reflective rose gold palettes trimming the hem, and best of all, tutu-type skirts that flared out as they spun around and around in the sunshine.

"Look, Mama! We're princesses!" I remember them calling out as they made themselves dizzy watching their skirts flare out, the palettes catching glints of sunlight. Oh their precious little faces! Lit up with joy and sunshine! They wanted to wear those dresses everywhere—school, church, the playground, the grocery store, while wrestling with their dad, even to sleep. Why? Because when they wore them, they felt special. They felt like the kinds of people they always wanted to be (beautiful princesses) but knew they couldn't be on their own.

Get this: The Hebrew for the word exult conveys not only rejoicing but also spinning around! Beloved, our garments of salvation, the ones Jesus Himself wrapped around us through His sacrifice on the cross. . . oh the beauty! If we could see them, I wager we'd all be spinning around and around in the sunshine, tears streaming down our faces with joy! Rise, my friend! Not only has He clothed you with such finery because He loves you, but also because He has a purpose for you. Adjust your headdress, my love, because you are a priest, employed by Him to serve His flock. Fasten that earring, darling, because He has promised Himself to you, to bring you the gift of being known and protected. We can't always know why He has given us another morning, but if He has given us one, then we must rise to the occasion!

> We can't always know why He has given us another morning, but . . . we must rise to the occasion!

As you prepare this decadent breakfast tonight to enjoy tomorrow morning, consider why God woke you up this morning. Think through three of your talents, three things that make you, you.

PRAY WITH ME

Father, sometimes it feels easier for me to stay in bed and hide under the covers than it is to get up and face the day. Sometimes it feels like even though I know I should rise and shine, I have no "shine" left to give. Thank You for this reminder that, because of Your sacrifice, I have every reason to rejoice! My circumstances may not be what I want, but wrapped in Your robes of salvation, I have every reason to rejoice anyway. Strengthen me to rise to the occasion You've set before me. Help me to see why You've put me here, and bless me with every little thing I need to complete the mission You've created for me. Thank You, Lord. Amen.

Banoffee French Toast Casserole

MAKES 6 TO 8 SERVINGS | **TOTAL TIME:** 9 HOURS | **ACTIVE TIME:** 25 MINUTES

2 cups whole milk, cold

½ cup canned dulce de leche, plus extra ¼ cup for drizzling

1 tablespoon instant coffee or espresso

5 large eggs, at room temperature

1 teaspoon vanilla extract

¼ teaspoon kosher salt

10 cups French bread or ciabatta, cut or torn into 1-inch cubes, crust on

1 stick (8 tablespoons) unsalted butter, plus extra softened butter for greasing

Pinch kosher salt

4 to 5 graham crackers, crumbled finely

1 pint whipping cream

Flaky salt

4 bananas, sliced into ½-inch rounds

1. Whisk ½ cup dulce de leche and ½ cup of milk together in a medium saucepan set over medium heat, just until well combined. Do not allow to simmer. Remove from heat. Whisk in remaining milk and instant coffee.

2. In a very large bowl, whisk together eggs, vanilla, and salt. Slowly add milk mixture, a little at a time, whisking constantly. Fold in the bread cubes, making sure to coat every piece.

3. Grease 8x11 baking dish with softened butter. Pour bread mixture into the dish. Cover with plastic wrap and refrigerate overnight.

4. The next day, preheat oven to 375 degrees Fahrenheit.

5. Set a small stainless steel skillet over medium heat. Cut 8 tablespoons of butter into 4 parts and add to the pan. Keep an eye on it, swirling often, and allow butter to melt, then bubble, then brown. As soon as it smells nutty, remove from heat. Drizzle 4 tablespoons of the browned butter over the top of the casserole. Bake, uncovered for 35 to 45 minutes, until the top is crispy.

6. Meanwhile, add graham cracker crumbs to remaining brown butter and set over a medium flame. Cook, stirring frequently, until crumbs crisp up. Season with a good pinch of salt and set aside.

7. Whip the cream to soft speaks. Refrigerate until ready to serve.

8. In the last 10 minutes of the baking,

warm the dulce de leche in the microwave or in a small saucepan over medium-low heat, until it's pouring consistency. Set aside. Slice bananas on the diagonal.

9. When casserole is ready, pull it out of the oven, and allow it to cool for about 10 minutes. Drizzle with extra dulce de leche and sprinkle with a handful of toasted graham cracker crumbs. Sprinkle with flaky salt.

10. Adorn servings of the casserole with dollops of whipped cream and a few slices of banana. Enjoy and shine!

CHAPTER 3

When You Need Hope

Do you recall the story of the Shunammite woman (II Kings 4:8-17)? A woman of great social and financial prominence, she also had the gift of empathic hospitality; she built an "upper chamber" onto her home so the prophet Elisha had a place to pray and rest his head. She was a capable, no-nonsense woman who used her smarts, standing, and wealth to fix nearly any issue.

And yet there was one problem she couldn't fix. When Elisha asked her how he could repay her generosity, she demurred, "I live among my own people." (In other words, she was all good.) Elisha's astute servant, Gehazi, then mentioned a dashed hope so disheartening that she didn't dare whisper it: She was childless. Elisha promised that she'd give birth the following year, and I can hear her voice cracking in reply.

"No, my lord, O man of God, do not lie to your maidservant."
II KINGS 4:16 NASB

Oh my friend. As someone who pined for a baby for years and was told she'd probably never have one, I relate to her response deeply. This woman had hoped before and had been disappointed. A sensible woman, she wouldn't let the pain of that disappointment demolish her faith in God. Instead, she'd put it in a box and buried it. The pain of that unanswered prayer was too much to bear. And now she was being asked to hope again.

Sometimes it feels easier to carry the burden of an unanswered prayer than to hold onto the hope that God will answer it.

Sometimes it feels like it takes an awful lot of courage to hope.

> She wouldn't let the pain of that disappointment demolish her faith in God.

And yet, when we commit our lives to Jesus, hope is our inheritance. This hope isn't wishful thinking. It's an expectation bolstered by confidence in the One from whom all good things come. It's an outlook based on the fact that we've read the last page of the book, and we know that the ending is good. Very, very good.

When the concept of hope stings, how do we coax ourselves to try again? Listen to the psalmist:

For You are my hope;
O Lord God, You are my confidence from my youth.
PSALM 71:5 NASB

Hope for the future is built on looking back at our past.

When we run out of the courage to hope, let's look at God's track record. That's why the Israelites built altars of remembrance—to encourage their faith in the hard times ahead. We recall God's faithfulness by looking in the rearview mirror. It gives us strength to drive forward, knowing that His hand is on the steering wheel.

> Hope isn't wishful thinking. It's an expectation bolstered by confidence in the One from whom all good things come.

The Shunammite woman had buried her hope, and yet the pain of that disappointment was close to the surface. Our hope isn't to be buried, because to do so begets a sense of self-preservation. But we aren't to preserve ourselves. Our Maker does that. And He wants to treat every part of us, even the parts that are hurt. Excavate that hope. Pull it out of the darkness and lay it before Jesus, our living hope. Just as it's out of character for Him to be a false hope, it's out of ours to be a hopeless people.

Dare to hope again, my friend, not because hope answered is the goal, but because hope satisfied in Him is our inheritance.

What prayer have you given up hope of God answering? As you make this delicious khachapuri, think of one time in your life that God has answered a deeply needed prayer. Talk to Him about it.

PRAY WITH ME

Jesus, we won't mince words here. Sometimes You disappoint us. It feels impossible to hold onto hope. But right now we remind our souls that You are good and faithful, and that if You've said no to something, it's for our good. And if You've said not yet, it's because You've got something even better in store for us. We remind ourselves of

Your faithfulness to us in the past, and we remind ourselves that ultimately, our future is secure because of Your sacrifice on the cross. One day every one of our hopes will be realized when we get to spend eternity with You. Until then, help us to know when to let go of things we hope for that aren't good for us, and when to courageously hold onto hope for those things You've promised us. Thank You, Jesus. Amen.

I was thinking about a khachapuri, a cheese and egg bread that is meant to be shared. I thought it might be applicable because the egg is buried beneath the cheese (as the Shunammite woman buried her hope), but given that she was a woman of hospitality, I think she'd like the idea that once the egg yolk and cheese have been whisked together, everyone pulls off a piece of the crust to dip into that rich sauce.

Chili Cheese Khachapuri

MAKES 2 TO 4 SERVINGS | **TOTAL TIME:** 2 HOURS 40 MINUTES | **ACTIVE TIME:** 20 MINUTES

Cook's Note: This is a conversation between an old love of mine, India's beloved chili cheese toast, and a new one, the Georgian breakfast classic, khachapuri. This traditional cheese and egg bread is designed to be shared, which I think the Shunammite woman, being a woman of hospitality, would appreciate. Encourage everyone at your table to rip off a bit of the crust and dip into that bright egg yolk. To me, the golden yolk symbolizes our hope, which we can sometimes bury but which is always waiting for us to rediscover and cling to in Christ.

12 ounces (340g) store-bought pizza dough

1 tablespoon extra virgin olive oil

1 cup (100g) shredded whole milk, low-moisture mozzarella cheese

⅓ cup (40g) goat cheese, finely crumbled

⅓ cup (40g) feta cheese, finely crumbled

2 large scallions, finely chopped

1 serrano or jalapeño chili, minced (seeds and membranes removed if you don't like heat)

2 teaspoons lime zest (from about 1 lime)

2 tablespoons ghee or unsalted butter, melted

1 large egg

1. Pour extra virgin olive oil into a large bowl, and coat sides with it. Place dough in the bowl, and toss to coat in oil. Cover with a damp cloth, and set in a warm place to rise until double in size, about 2 hours. If your counters get cold, place a folded kitchen towel underneath the bowl.

2. Heat oven to 450 degrees. Line a baking sheet with parchment paper; set aside. On a lightly floured surface, stretch and roll dough into a circle, ¼-inch thick, 10 to 12 inches across. Brush off excess flour, then lay the dough on the sheet tray. Using your fingers, create a wall around the perimeter of the circle by rolling the edge in on itself. The wall should be about ½-inch thick. Then, press and pinch the narrow ends together to form two points. Your dough should look like a boat or an eye-shape. Allow to rest in a warm place while you prepare the filling.

3. Tumble cheeses, scallions, chile and lime zest into a medium bowl. Add 3 tablespoons water. Stir together with a fork until well combined. Scrape cheese mixture into center of the khachapuri, making sure to create an even layer.

4. Pop into the oven, and bake until crust begins to brown, about 15 minutes. Then, make an indentation in the middle. Crack egg into it. Brush sides with melted ghee, and sprinkle with a little salt. Return khachapuri to the oven for 8 minutes until the white is set. Serve hot, encouraging everyone to rip pieces off the rim and drip into the gooey yolk and cheese mixture!

CHAPTER 4

When You Need Good News

I walked out to inspect my raised garden beds and gasped audibly. "What happened to you, my baby?" I cried. (I am a little obsessive when it comes to my plant babies.) One of my tomato vines had collapsed on itself, probably dealt a lethal blow by the neighborhood cat or raccoon, right near the base of the stem. My daughters and I leaped into action. They looked for a strong stick, and I went inside to grab some kitchen twine and scissors. We planted the stick right next to the tomato plant, lifted her back up, and then as the girls held her upright, I gently tied the two together. Within minutes, what had looked like the end for my cherry tomatoes was a new beginning, another chance at producing the sugary-sweet fruit for which she's named.

Do you feel like my tomato plant sometimes? Has life knocked you down one too many times, and you're crying out for someone or something to pick you up?

> *Be strong, and let your heart take courage,*
> *all you who wait for the LORD!*
> PSALM 31:24 ESV

This verse wraps up a psalm of David, where he talks himself out of anguish into assurance, and this is a significant ending. It mirrors God's words to Joshua before taking down the walls of Jericho, and this wording is used nearly 20 times in the Old Testament, usually before a battle. This verse girds our loins, because it reminds us that to be strong, we must stand firm, we must hold strongly with God. Much like the stick and twine held up my sweet little tomato plant, our strengths come from binding

He will give you strength to withstand whatever battle may be ahead.

ourselves to God's power. Only then will we have courage. So as you wait on good news, my darling, wrap your arms around Jesus. He will give you strength to withstand whatever battle may be ahead and produce the good fruit He made you to produce!

Blistered Tomato Toasts
with Whipped Feta

MAKES 4 SERVINGS | **TOTAL TIME:** 40 MINUTES | **ACTIVE TIME:** 20 MINUTES

2 tablespoons avocado oil, plus more for brushing on bread

1 pint cherry or grape tomatoes

2 cloves garlic, minced

½-inch piece ginger, minced

¼ teaspoon cumin seeds, chopped

¼ teaspoon white granulated sugar

¼ teaspoon apple cider vinegar

Kosher salt (diamond crystal) and freshly ground black pepper

4 (1-inch thick) slices of good hearty bread, such as sourdough or country loaf

4 ounces feta cheese

6 tablespoons full-fat plain greek yogurt

1 tablespoon extra virgin olive oil

1 lemon, cut into wedges

1 jalapeño chili, sliced into thin rounds

1. Adjust oven rack to the center of the oven, then set to 425 degrees Fahrenheit.

2. In large bowl, toss together 2 tablespoons oil, tomatoes, garlic, ginger, cumin seeds, sugar, apple cider vinegar, ½ teaspoon kosher salt, and a few grinds of black pepper. Massage the ingredients into each other.

3. Pour onto a parchment or foil-lined baking sheet and roast, shaking every now and then, for 15 to 20 minutes or until tomatoes are wilted. Remove the pan and allow to cool.

4. Meanwhile, brush bread with a little oil, and season with salt and pepper. Bake until the bread is turning golden brown in spots, about 5 minutes. Transfer to cutting board.

5. Make whipped feta: Blend feta cheese and yogurt in a blender or food processor until smooth. Now add olive oil and blend until incorporated. Taste and adjust seasoning to your palate.

6. To serve, first smush down tomatoes so they open up a little. Spoon a little whipped feta on a slice of bread, swooshing it around with the back of a spoon. Then, spoon some roasted tomato on top, followed by a squeeze of lemon. Finish with a couple rounds of sliced jalapeño. Repeat with remaining toasts and serve!

CHAPTER 5

When You Need Love

I was eleven when I began to believe that I was unlovable. It's a bit of a long story—one of those middle school experiences where you suddenly realize that you're not paranoid; everyone you care about does indeed hate you. Thirty years and months of therapy later, I'm just starting to get over it.

Beloved, are you feeling unloved or unlovable today?

We all do at times. And to understand why, we have to start at the beginning. We were all made by God, whom the disciple John called love itself.

> *Beloved . . . everyone who loves is born of God and knows God.*
> *The one who does not love does not know God, for God is love.*
> I JOHN 4:7-8 NASB

Love fashioned us out of dust. Love blew His spirit into us. Love dreamed a story for each of us, and Love is seeing it to completion. We are the descendants of Love, and thus He designed us to be sustained by a specific love only He can give us, something the ancient Greeks called agape.

Agape is the benevolent, self-sacrificial love of God for humanity. It's a feeling, yes, but it's also a choice to work for our well-being, even if it's at His expense, even if it might be rejected, even if it has been rejected. Agape doesn't love the way we do—based on either logical quid pro quo or on mercurial affections. Agape loves because it's agape. God loves because . . . God loves.

> We were all made by God, whom the disciple John called love itself.

To me, the whole story of the Bible is that of humanity rejecting God and then trying to exist on the love of romantic partners, sons and daughters, family, friends, work mates, and even strangers. And while we might seem fed, our stomachs still growl because we're malnourished. We're missing the one vital nutrient that only God can give us: agape.

But God doesn't abandon us to our hunger. Instead, out of His agape for us, He chases after us and commits the most profound act of love ever. As Jesus puts it,

"Greater love has no one than this,
than to lay down one's life for his friends."
JOHN 15:13 NKJV

> Love fashioned us out of dust. Love blew His spirit into us. Love dreamed a story for each of us.

And so, my friend, when you and I feel unloved, when we feel unseen or forgotten, let's return to the source of all love in the universe. Let's speak to our souls. I talk to my soul a lot. "O my soul," I say, "don't forget that Someone loved you so much, and wanted you back so much, that He allowed Himself to be tortured and sacrificed just so you could know His love for you."

When we mimic Jesus, selflessly loving others, we grow in intimacy with Him. We understand His character more, and thus taste the love He has for us.

Essentially, if we need more agape, we need to practice some agape.

The early church understood this, holding what they called "agape feasts" or "love feasts," a communal meal that's still practiced by some denominations today. The following recipe is purposefully written to share with whomever God puts on your heart.

God loves you, beloved. He loves you with a passion so intense that nothing on earth can compare to it. Love made us. Love sustains us. Love died for us. And if we want to experience more of that love, we can find it in extending some love to those God has put in our path. Or, as John so beautifully puts it, "No one has ever seen God; if we love one another, God abides in us and his love is perfected in us" (I John 4:12 ESV).

As you make your rock cakes today, listen to Jess Ray's song "Runaway." Does this remind you of how God chased you down? Ask God to show you someone who needs to feel God's love right now. When will you make this dish and take it to them? Make a commitment.

PRAY WITH ME

Lord, thank You for Your great love for me, for leaving the ninety-nine to find me. Bless this endeavor to share Your love with _____. I do this because I am a child of love. Please use it for Your purposes, and help me to understand You more intimately through this simple act. Amen.

He loves you with a passion so intense that nothing on earth can compare to it.

Rock Cakes and Masala Chai

MAKES ABOUT 30 | **TOTAL TIME:** 1 HOUR 10 MINUTES | **ACTIVE TIME:** 30 MINUTES

Rock Cakes

2 cups (320g) golden raisins/
sultanas

1 cup brandy or orange juice

4 cups (600g) all-purpose
flour

1 cup (200g) granulated cane
or white sugar, plus extra for
sprinkling

2 tablespoons (24g) baking
powder

1 teaspoon ground
cardamom

1 teaspoon fine sea salt

2 large eggs

⅔ cup whole milk, plus more
as needed

1½ tablespoons vanilla
extract

16 tablespoons (226g) cold
unsalted butter, chopped

2 teaspoons fresh orange
zest (from about 2 large
oranges)

1. Preheat oven to 400 degrees Fahrenheit. Line 3 sheet pans with parchment paper.

2. Mix golden raisins and brandy together in a small bowl. Microwave on high for 1 minutes, then stir, and allow to sit for 15 minutes. Drain and set aside.

3. Sift flour, sugar, baking powder, cardamom, and salt into a large bowl. Separately, whisk eggs, milk, and vanilla extract together in a measuring cup.

4. Add cold butter cubes. Now, using your fingertips, rub in the butter until the mixture resembles breadcrumbs.

5. Make well in the center, then pour in the egg mixture. Use a wooden spoon to stir until the mixture just comes together as a thick, lumpy dough. If it's not coming together, add a teaspoon or two more milk. Stir in raisins, making sure they are well distributed.

6. Using either a #24/1.67 ounce ice cream scoop or your eyes, place 10 golfball-sized dollops of rock cake mixture on each prepared baking sheet, being sure to leave room between them to grow. You should get about 30 rock cakes. Sprinkle each cake with a little extra sugar.

7. Bake for 15 to 20 minutes (in batches if necessary), until golden brown on the bottom and a little on top too; their internal temperature should register 200 degrees Fahrenheit. Cool rock cakes on sheet pans for 5 minutes, then transfer to wire racks to cool. These are at their best when served warm. Now make some chai!

Masala Chai

MAKES 2 SERVINGS | **TOTAL TIME:** 15 MINUTES | **ACTIVE TIME:** 10 MINUTES

4 to 5 green cardamom pods

4 whole black peppercorns

½-inch piece cinnamon

3 whole cloves

¾-inch piece peeled, fresh ginger, sliced

Pinch of salt

3 teaspoons loose leaf black tea, or 3 tea bags, preferably Assam tea

¾ cup milk of choice (recommended: whole milk or full-fat oat milk)

Sweetener of choice (recommended: honey)

1. Place a medium saucepan over medium heat. Add cardamom pods, black peppercorns, cinnamon stick, and cloves in the saucepan and toast, stirring and shaking the saucepan until fragrant, about 1 minute. Shake the spices into a mortar and pestle; add ginger, and bash them all up until the cardamom pods are open and the ginger releases its fragrance. It doesn't need to be a paste, just a coarse mash.

2. Scoop the mixture back into the saucepan and cover with 2 cups of water. Cover and bring to a boil.

3. Now add black tea. Turn heat off, cover and allow to steep for 3 to 5 minutes, depending on how strong you like your tea.

4. Add milk, and bring to a boil, uncovered. Once it boils, let it boil a few seconds longer—the contents should start to climb up the sides of the saucepan. Cut the heat before it bubbles over!

    Add your sweetener of choice and then strain into mugs. Allow to cool before taking your first sip!

CHAPTER 6

When You Need Faith

When my own trust in God has wavered, something in me has imagined Jesus saying something like this:

"I find your lack of faith disturbing."—Darth Vader

Thankfully the Jesus of my imagination bears very little resemblance to the Jesus of the Bible! Remember this beauty?

> *"I tell you the truth, if you had faith even as small as a mustard seed, you could say to this mountain, 'Move from here to there,' and it would move."*
>
> MATTHEW 17:20 NLT

Comparing something to a mustard seed was a Jewish idiom that meant "the smallest of things." Conversely, to compare something to the mountains conveyed the insurmountable nature of things.

And so Jesus was saying, "Even when you bring Me your smallest scrap of faith, it's enough for Me to make the impossible . . . possible."

The size and strength of our faith is not the driving force of change. The quality and the object of our faith is. What does that mean?

Well, while the mustard seed is indeed one of the smallest seeds in the vegetable kingdom, try popping one in your mouth. It's a fiery little one, isn't it? Mustard makes no apologies for her intensity. She doesn't disguise herself. One bite and a little firework jets up your nostrils, announcing, "I'm here!" Let our faith be the same way, my friend. Once sparked by adversity, let it spark into action, unapologetic and unchanging in the intensity of its identity as tethered to Christ. That's some quality faith!

As to the object of our faith, consider the mustard tree. At first, her delicate shoots are susceptible to

> By stretching out our hands toward heaven, by focusing on God as the source of our living water, we grow stronger.

wind, sun, birds, and rocky soil. Over time, her roots stretch deeply through the soil, searching for the living water she knows will cause her to blossom. In fact, mustard trees are known to have some of the deepest and strongest root systems around!

So too for us; by stretching out our hands toward heaven, by focusing on God as the source of our living water, we grow stronger. Not only are we able to withstand the wind, sun, and birds that previously struck fear in our hearts, but now the birds themselves also make nests in our boughs! By focusing on God, we take our eyes off our own powerlessness, and instead bask in the warmth and glory of El Shaddai, the Mighty One. By drawing down, we stretch up and out, extending our branches to those around us, giving them shelter from the elements under our leafy arms, feeding them with the fruit God brings to bear, and encouraging them with our faithful witness to His faithfulness.

> I draw toward You, Jesus, the object and the replenisher of my faith.

Whenever my faith flounders, I examine my root system. Is it in a state of drought? Is there a thin layer of dust on my Bible? Do the walls of my home ache for some worship music? Do I need to call a sibling in Christ?

While Darth Vader might find our paltry offering of faith disturbing, Jesus expects it from us! He's much more interested in the quality than the quantity. Bring what little you have to the altar, darlin'. Water it with time spent with Him, and He will cause it to grow and blossom!

YOUR TURN

Close your eyes and take a small bite of mustard. Experience it dancing across your palate, up your nose, and maybe even tingling your eyes! How does your faith compare? Does it need refreshing? Does it have a fragrant aroma (Philippians 4:18)? Does it make your eyes water?

PRAY WITH ME

Father, thank You so much for the gift of faith. Some days it feels like I have bushels of it, but today, it feels like a mustard seed's worth. I draw toward You, Jesus, the object and the replenisher of my faith. I know You love to give good gifts, and so please would You give me the great gift of a deeper, stronger faith in You? I cannot do it without You. I love You! Amen.

Turkish Eggs (Cilbir) with Pickled Mustard Seeds

MAKES 2 TO 3 SERVINGS | **TOTAL TIME:** 50 MINUTES | **ACTIVE TIME:** 35 MINUTES

½ cup black or brown mustard seeds

¾ cup white wine vinegar, plus ¼ cup

½ teaspoon kosher salt

2 tablespoons honey

1 cup full-fat plain greek yogurt, left at room temperature for 20 minutes (don't skip this step!)

1 clove garlic, peeled and grated

2 tablespoons minced fresh dill, plus extra picked feathery stands for garnish

2 tablespoons minced fresh mint, plus extra leaves for garnish

½ stick unsalted butter

1 tablespoon Aleppo pepper (or 1 teaspoon red chili flakes + 2 teaspoons sweet paprika)

2 large, cold eggs

2 tablespoons rice wine vinegar, or other lightly flavored vinegar

Kosher salt and pepper

Persian or English cucumbers, diagonally sliced, for serving

2 slices toasted bread

1. Make pickled mustard seeds: Place mustard seeds in a small saucepan. Cover with water, and bring to a boil, then drain through a fine-mesh strainer. Repeat 2 more times (this removes excess bitterness). Tip mustard seeds back into the saucepan. Cover with ¾ cup of white wine vinegar, salt, and honey. Bring to a simmer over medium-high heat, then turn down to low and simmer for 20 minutes, stirring occasionally.

2. Remove the saucepan from the heat and allow to cool to room temperature. Add remaining vinegar, and pour into airtight glass jar. Pickled mustard seeds will keep in the fridge for about 3 months.

3. Stir yogurt well with a spoon or whisk until smooth. Add garlic, minced dill, and minced mint, season with salt and pepper; stir until combined. Taste for seasoning, and set aside.

4. Melt butter in a skillet over medium heat, until it starts to pop. Now add the Aleppo pepper and a pinch of salt. Cook for about 30 seconds to 1 minute, until fragrant. Take off heat, and set aside.

5. Fill a large saucepan halfway with water, and bring to a gentle simmer. Meanwhile, set a strainer over a bowl. Crack an egg into it, allowing the runny white to drain through the strainer, leaving the yolk and the more structured white behind. Pop this part of the egg into a small cup or teacup and discard the runny whites. Repeat process with remaining egg, dropping it into its own cup and discarding the runny whites.

6. Add vinegar to the simmering water. Turn the heat off. Swirl a wooden spoon in a circle in the water, creating a whirlpool effect. Quickly drop both eggs in at the same time—the swirling current will help the egg whites wrap around the yolk. Allow to sit, undisturbed, for 3 to 4 minutes until white is set up but yolk is still soft. Remove with a slotted spoon to a paper towel-lined plate.

To serve: spoon yogurt into a shallow bowl, and swoosh it around with the back of your spoon, creating ridges and valleys but a fairly flat middle spot to land your eggs. Spoon a few spoonfuls of the Aleppo butter over the yogurt. Add the eggs, drizzle with a touch more Aleppo butter. Shower with fresh herbs, then carefully dollop little servings of pickled mustard seeds around the bowl too. Serve immediately with sliced cucumbers and toasted bread.

CHAPTER 7

When You Need Kindness

O ne day, a friend of mine and I were shooting a show together. I offered to show her how to go live on Instagram so we could promote her latest cookbook.

"I'm so sorry I'm late!" I huffed, as I climbed into her trailer. I explained that I'd been painstakingly typing my Butter Chicken recipe onto my cell phone because I'd just lost my laptop. Buying a new one was out of the budget, so my cell phone would have to do. She tutted about it being a shame, and we got on with the live Instagram lesson.

The next day, an email in my inbox announced that a laptop was on its way to my house. I texted my husband.

"Did you buy a laptop, hon?"

"No, I was about to ask you the same thing because one just arrived on our doorstep!" he replied.

I suddenly remembered how my friend had slyly asked for my address, which I assumed had been for her cookbook. I texted her. "Did you just send me a laptop?!"

"You write good words. The world needs to hear them," she wrote back.

I wept. It was an extremely generous gift, yes. But also, her kindness communicated that she saw me and she believed in me. It said, *You don't have to do this alone. I see you, and I'm in your corner.* I'll never forget that gift. In fact, I'm typing to you on it right now! Isn't that incredible?

In our competitive, dog-eat-dog, survival-of-the-fittest world, kindness doesn't make sense. Kindness means handicapping ourselves in order to give someone else an advantage. It knocks the breath out of us when we experience it, because it's so counter-cultural, so unexpected. And in my eyes? It's just so . . . God.

My favorite story of kindness in the Scriptures is II Samuel 9. The newly crowned King David wants to keep the covenant he had made to Jonathan, son of the previous king, Saul, who had tried to kill David. The covenant had declared a lasting peace between the two warring families—a way to bury the hatchet, so to speak.

David asks, "Is there not yet anyone of the house of Saul to whom I may show the kindness of God?" (II Samuel 9:3 NASB)

Enter Mephibosheth (II Samuel 9:6), Jonathan's crippled son. Ancient custom would have allowed David to massacre anyone connected to the previous reign. Mephibosheth, who was lame, approached with dread, assuming that death was on the table. Instead, David invited him to a table of reconciliation. David honored him by bringing him into the royal palace and providing for his daily needs. He even restored his birthright: his grandfather Saul's estate! Instead of revenge, David chose kindness. He gave Mephibosheth dignity and a new identity as friend of the king.

Do you see how this echoes our own relationship with God? So often, humanity stands in opposition to God, choosing our own way over His. Paul even goes so far as to call us "enemies" of God (Romans 5:10). Like David, God has every right to defeat His enemies and yet, because He is kindness itself, He chooses mercy. Not only does He forgive us, He redefines us as His sons and daughters. Wow! The Hebrew word *hesed* is used interchangeably for both words. Why? Well, mercy is showing forgiveness when you could show punishment, which is an act of kindness. Mercy and kindness feed each other, and they empower the ultimate act of kindness to humanity: the cross.

Sometimes when I need kindness, I'll chastise myself. The cross is the most kindness anyone has ever shown me, so shouldn't I be satisfied with that? How dare I ask for me! And while that's somewhat true, God's kindness doesn't end there.

> *"For the mountains may depart and the hills be removed, but my*
> *steadfast love shall not depart from you, and my covenant of peace*
> *shall not be removed," says the LORD, who has compassion on you.*
> ISAIAH 54:10 ESV

His kindness didn't end at the cross. That's just where it began, and guess what? It's never-ending! There will be times when the people and the things you thought were as steadfast as the mountains will let you down. And you will look around for kindness. "Does anyone see me in my distress?"

Yes, dear one. God sees you. Like Mephibosheth, your new identity and birthright are in His hands, and He longs to give it to you!

I will forever think of my friend's kindness when I make Butter Chicken. There's an extravagance to kindness—a sense that while it wasn't necessary on paper, it's the very thing your soul was craving. Butter Chicken, that traditional, decadent Indian dish is my kind of soul food. And so I bring you a modernized soul food classic: Butter Chicken and Waffles.

Butter Chicken and Waffle Sandwich

MAKES 4 SERVINGS | **TOTAL TIME:** 26 HOURS | **ACTIVE TIME:** 1 HOUR 15 MINUTES

Cook's Note: This recipe is a *lot*, but I can see this being a fun Saturday project with someone you love! To make ginger garlic paste, toss peeled ginger and garlic (1½ cups each) into a food processor. Add white vinegar (¼ cup for 3 cups total ginger and garlic) and a good pinch of salt. Pour into a jar and it should stay fresh, in your fridge, for about 3 weeks. Tandoori seasoning is a heady blend of spices; for this recipe, store-bought is fine. You can also substitute 2 teaspoons sweet paprika + 1 teaspoon garam masala for every tablespoon of tandoori seasoning.

Fried Chicken:

1 cup whole milk buttermilk

1 tablespoon homemade or store-bought ginger-garlic paste (see Cook's Note)

Kosher salt

1 teaspoon granulated cane or white sugar

1 tablespoon ghee

2 tablespoons store-bought tandoori seasoning (recommended: Shan brand), divided

1½ pounds boneless skinless chicken thighs, trimmed of excess fat

Peanut or canola oil for deep frying

1½ cups all purpose flour

½ cup cornstarch

1 teaspoon baking powder

Gravy:

2 tablespoons avocado or other neutral oil

3 tablespoons cold unsalted butter, divided

½ teaspoon whole cumin seed

2 dried bay leaves

½ large onion, finely diced (about 150g)

1 tablespoons ginger-garlic paste

1½ teaspoons tandoori seasoning

1 14-ounce can crushed tomatoes, fire-roasted ideally

¼ cup (38g) whole raw cashews

1 teaspoons granulated cane or white sugar

½ teaspoon apple cider vinegar

½ teaspoon dried fenugreek leaves (optional)

¾ cup heavy cream

Waffles:

1 28-ounce box waffle mix

Eggs

2 scallions, minced

1½ tablespoons minced ginger

2 teaspoons cumin seeds, toasted

Handful of cilantro leaves and soft stems, coarsely chopped

2 limes, sliced into wedges

1. The night before or the morning of, brine the chicken: Whisk buttermilk, ginger-garlic paste, 2 teaspoons kosher salt and sugar together in a large bowl or storage container. Spoon 1 tablespoon tandoori seasoning on the surface of the buttermilk. Warm ghee in a small saucepan until hot, then pour over the tandoori seasoning. It should sizzle! Stir together. Add chicken to the buttermilk brine, making sure to coat each piece. Cover and refrigerate for 4 to 24 hours.

2. Make the gravy: Set medium saucepan over medium heat. Add oil and 1 tablespoon butter and warm until shimmering. Now add the cumin seeds and bay leaves. Once seeds darken and release their fragrance (10 to 20 seconds), add the onion. Cook, stirring often, until just starting to turn golden brown, 8 to 10 minutes.

3. Add ginger-garlic, tandoori seasoning and a splash of water. Cook until the raw fragrance dissipates, about 1 minute.

4. Now pour in crushed tomatoes and their juices, cashews and ½ teaspoon kosher salt, 1 teaspoon sugar, and apple cider vinegar. Stir well, and bring it all to a boil over high heat. Then, turn heat down to low and simmer, uncovered, for 15 to 20 until thickened. Stir every now and then to ensure nothing sticks.

5. Pull out bay leaves. Pour tomato mixture into a blender and puree with ¼ cup water until smooth. Return to pan, adding a little more water if the sauce looks too thick.

6. Crumble in the dried fenugreek leaves, then stir in heavy cream. Now stir in remaining cold butter. Taste for seasoning, adjusting to your palate. Set aside.

7. Fry chicken: fill a 10-inch cast iron skillet with peanut or canola oil to a 1-inch depth. Set over medium-high heat, and heat to 375 degrees Fahrenheit.

8. Whisk flour, cornstarch, baking powder, 1 tablespoon tandoori seasoning and 1 teaspoon salt together in a large bowl. Set aside. Set wire racks in 2 sheet pans. Preheat oven to 200 degrees.

9. Time to fry! With one hand, remove one piece of chicken from the buttermilk brine, allowing excess to drip off. Drop into flour mixture. With the other hand, toss to coat evenly and then transfer to one of the rack-lined baking sheets. Repeat with remaining chicken.

10. When oil is ready, carefully place 3 to 4 thighs in the pan. Cook, turning every 1 to 2 minutes, until deep brown on each side and the center registers 160 degrees Fahrenheit, about 5 minutes per side. Land chicken on the other prepared sheet pan, and set in oven to stay warm as you make the waffles.

11. Follow instructions on the waffle mix to make 4 to 5 waffles. Add minced scallions, ginger, and cumin seeds to the batter. Prepare waffles on your waffle iron (I like to use a mini iron!).

12. To assemble, spread a little gravy on one waffle. Top with a piece of chicken and a small handful of cilantro. Squeeze a wedge of lime over the top. Top with another waffle. Serve immediately!

CHAPTER 8

When You Need Goodness

Recently, it has felt like one difficulty after another has befallen my family, but the hardest of all has been the return of a disease that God healed Brendan of in his childhood. The reprise hit us hard, not only physically but also spiritually: where was God's goodness in this?

It's one thing to know that the oft-prescribed Romans 8:28 is true: God is good—how can He not be? He's only one *O* away from good—and I do believe that He is working all things for His glory and for the good of those who love Him.

But good is abstract, isn't it? It's theoretical, a shared belief about God's nature that we build our foundation upon. When I'm struggling to see evidence of God's good work, I find it hard to keep building on that foundation.

Where do we start when we're searching for His fingerprint on the mess and turmoil surrounding us?

Let's go back to Romans 8:28:

> *We know that for those who love God all things work together for good, for those who are called according to his purpose. (ESV)*

Our Father's power is not only paramount, unmitigated, and absolute, but it's always exerted for more and more good on humanity. Since our understanding of "good" was forever skewed by the cataclysm in the Garden, sometimes what is good for us tastes like death on our palates. It makes me think of fermented foods like kimchi and sauerkraut, foods that are literally in the process of dying and yet, ironically, are full of life-giving bacteria, the very bacteria that many of us need in order to live full, healthy lives. Some of these foods are an acquired taste, and yet cultures around the world have, for centuries, recognized how vital they are not only for our survival but for our blossoming!

> He is working all things for His glory, and for the good of those who love Him.

> My friend, the evidence for goodness in our lives is sometimes the very bitterness on our palates.

My friend, the evidence for goodness in our lives is sometimes the very bitterness on our palates. Taste and see that the Lord is good!

Praise God that while He sits on the throne above us, He is also sitting down here on the floor with us. He understands us better than we even understand ourselves. He knows that we need reminders that His "invisible" hand is always at work for us.

Think back to the Israelites wandering in the desert after He set them free from slavery to the Egyptians. In Exodus 33, God told Moses that it was time to move, and he responded:

> *Moses said to the Lord, "You have been telling me, 'Lead these people,' but You have not let me know whom You will send with me. . . . If You are pleased with me, teach me Your ways so I may know You and continue to find favor with You. Remember that this nation is Your people."*
>
> EXODUS 33:12-13 NIV

Did you catch that? Moses said he'd like to see the whole roadmap so that he could know God. Is there a possibility he meant, "so I can trust that this plan is good enough"? I see myself in Moses at this moment, do you? Even though Moses' request might be a bit impertinent, God, in His sweetness, promises:

> *"I will cause all My goodness to pass in front of you."*
>
> EXODUS 33:19 NIV

God wouldn't show Moses the whole plan, probably because He knew Moses wouldn't be able to fully comprehend it. But He would reassure Moses that he was on the right path.

Generations later, David would recognize that same promise from God, in the famous twenty-third psalm:

> *Surely goodness and lovingkindness will follow me all the days of my life.*
>
> PSALM 23:6 NASB

As children of God, goodness is our constant companion.

If you are looking for evidence of good in your life right now, be empowered by the truth that what you're seeking is already there! It might be small, like the way

Bren's condition has encouraged our family to make healthier choices when it comes to our diet. Or it might be mighty, like the way our girls have watched their dad model what it looks like to praise God even in difficulty because faith in God doesn't mean a life free of trouble (or as Bren sometimes says, God isn't a vending machine). They understand this in a way we could never teach them.

And yet, I know sometimes that isn't satisfactory. So I'll leave you with this thought by another psalmist, Asaph. He recognized that since God is goodness, if he needed goodness, he needed to spend time with Him.

But as for me, the nearness of God is my good.
PSALM 73:28 NASB

There is nothing that satisfies the hunger of our souls more completely than the presence of God.

Make some quiet time now before you cook. Just as Moses did, find yourself a place far from the crowd—your own "tent of meeting." Play your favorite music that reminds you of God, or sit in silence. Read the following passage, a declaration from God Himself about who He is, the very words He declared to Moses and the Israelites in the wilderness. They remind us that even if life tastes like bitterness and death, God, in His goodness, will turn that death into life.

> Praise God that while He sits on the throne above us, He is also sitting down here on the floor with us.

Behold, I make a covenant. Before all your people I will do marvels such as have not been done in all the earth, nor in any nation; and all the people among whom you are shall see the work of the LORD. For it is an awesome thing that I will do with you.
EXODUS 34:10 NKJV

I turn to these Korean-style Vegetable Pancakes when random bits and pieces occupy my crisper drawer; a nubbin of carrot here, a hunk of cabbage there, the ubiquitous zucchini. I always eat mine with a mound of kimchi, the funky tang reminding me that if letting foods ferment can replenish my gut bacteria, surely God can work goodness out of the struggles of life.

Korean-style Vegetable Pancakes

MAKES 2 TO 3 SERVINGS | TOTAL TIME: 35 MINUTES | ACTIVE TIME: 35 MINUTES

Cook's Note: If scallions are particularly thick, slice in half lengthwise before cutting into 1-inch lengths. If you can't find rice flour, substitute with more all-purpose flour.

½ cup (75g) all-purpose flour

¼ cup (45g) rice flour

2 tablespoons cornstarch

½ teaspoon baking powder

½ teaspoon kosher salt

¾ cup ice-cold club soda or water

5 medium scallions (50g), white and green parts sliced into 1-inch lengths (see Cook's Note)

2 cups of various vegetables, sliced into matchsticks or grated (e.g., carrots, parsnips, zucchini, golden beets, celery root, mushrooms, etc.)

Avocado oil

Kimchi to serve alongside

Dipping sauce:

3 tablespoons soy sauce

1 tablespoon rice vinegar

1 tablespoon water

1 teaspoon toasted sesame seeds

¼ teaspoon toasted sesame oil

1. In a large bowl, whisk together all-purpose flour, rice flour, cornstarch and baking powder. Stir in club soda or water, stirring until a batter just comes together.

2. Now fold in all the vegetables, adding more club soda if necessary, to form a thick batter. It should look like more vegetables than batter, with the batter clinging to the vegetables. Set aside in the fridge while you make the dipping sauce.

3. In a medium bowl, whisk together soy sauce, rice vinegar, water, sesame seeds, and sesame oil. Taste for seasoning and set aside.

4. Preheat oven to 200 degrees Fahrenheit. Line a half sheet pan with paper towels, and set a wire rack in it.

5. Pour 2 teaspoons oil into an 8-inch nonstick skillet, and set over medium heat. Once shimmering, add ½ cup of mixture. Use the back of a spoon to flatten the mixture to a 6 to 7-inch round. Cook 2 to 3 minutes until golden brown to dark brown in spots on the bottom. Flip and cook on remaining side. Remove to prepared sheet pan, and repeat with remaining batter.

6. Serve with dipping sauce and kimchi.

CHAPTER 9

When You Need Purpose

There were two pretend games I played the most when I was little: cooking show host and news anchor. I'd set up my cooking set and walk the invisible cameras through a recipe, or those same cameras would follow me to the dining table where I'd read aloud from the newspaper, throwing my voice into my chest so I'd sound like the presenters I'd watched on the BBC World Service. I come from a pretty traditional Indian family, so choosing a career was massively important. I'm only two generations away from my grandfather, whose life as a rice farmer meant that one bad rainy season could wash away an entire crop, and with it, that year's income. When that's your recent history, finding a career that provides for your family in a stable and prosperous fashion becomes tantamount, and so, when it came time for me to choose my path, I let go of the cooking show host dream and picked up the journalism one. Eventually, God in His wisdom and sweetness gave me my first dream back.

But between the two, there was a waiting room where I was neither. I was unemployed. And for someone who had so deeply aligned her purpose with her career, it was devastating. Without purpose, I felt like a rudderless boat out to sea, floating along with no map, no sail plan, no power to even row because I didn't know which direction to row in. Life felt meaningless.

I wonder whether Simon Peter, the rock of the church, felt this way, especially in the dark days between Jesus' death and His resurrection. He'd walked away from a prosperous fishing business to follow Jesus of Nazareth. He'd risked his livelihood and his reputation following this rabble-rouser around Israel! And now, the man he'd believed was God in human trappings, was dead. Anyone associated with Jesus faced increasing hostility. I'd felt like my life was meaningless when I'd lost my career. Imagine how Peter felt after losing God?!

> God in His wisdom and sweetness gave me my first dream back.

This is why I particularly love this verse from the first letter of Peter, written to followers of The Way in the wake of Rome burning to the ground, and its emperor, Nero, subsequently scapegoating Christians for the disaster. Peter reminds them of their identity and their purpose:

> *"But you are a chosen race, a royal priesthood, a holy nation, a*
> *people for his possession, so that you may proclaim the praises of*
> *the one who called you out of darkness into his marvelous light."*
>
> I PETER 2:9 CSB

God has chosen you and me, friend, for a very high calling. Being born again secures our salvation, yes. But it also changes our identity. Where once we may have preeminently defined ourselves by our ancestry, skin color, language, profession, social class, or abilities, now our chief identity is "chosen by God."

We're a people group not defined by our past, but by our future;

Not by who we are, but by Whose;

Not by our talents, but by our calling.

We stand as the royal priesthood, liaisons between heaven and earth, a foot planted in each realm, calling all those living in the darkness that we once called home, to our new home in the light. I think back to the intricate robes God designed for the high priest in ancient Israel. The hemlines were adorned with gold bells interspersed with pomegranates fashioned out of scarlet, blue, and purple thread. The bells announced the priest's arrival, reminding everyone of his solemn purpose as emissary of God. The pomegranates were a reminder of the sweetness of our God, and to me, a foreshadowing of the forthcoming sacrifice of Christ. In order for the hundreds of seeds inside the pomegranate to fly and take root and prosper, the fruit has to die, to be ripped open, ruby red juice flowing to the ground.

God has chosen you and me, friend, for a very high calling.

One of my favorite stories is of the writer Robert Louis Stevenson, who as a young boy, loved watching the streetlamps come on as night fell. Before the days of electricity, a lamplighter would have to climb a ladder, lift the glass lid to light the gas torch, replace the lid and climb back down the ladder. It was slow. And yet, Stevenson was filled with joy as he watched, exclaiming, "Look! They're punching holes in the darkness!"

THAT is our true purpose, my friend! It isn't our career, our bank account, our marital or parental status, or how many people follow us on Instagram. Our purpose is to punch light into the darkness. And we do that by remaining in such a state of joy over the great work God did to rescue us, that we can't help but proclaim it to anyone we run into! We walk into every room, not just as ourselves, but in priestly garments adorned with tinkling gold bells and ruby-

Our purpose is to punch light into the darkness.

red pomegranates, bursting with the sweet fruit of the Gospel. In a way, each one of us is like a pomegranate; we bear the potential to spread hundreds and hundreds of good seeds as we travel along.

You aren't just anybody, darling. You are chosen. You are called. You are a treasured possession of the Lord, and your purpose is not to keep that status to yourself, but to invite others into it. You and I are lamplighters. Let's go punch some light.

Pomegranate parfait

Cook's Note: Pomegranate molasses is usually available alongside other Middle Eastern ingredients in the international aisle of the grocery store. It's also easily made at home by boiling down pure, unsweetened pomegranate juice with some sugar!

1 orange

⅔ cup honey

¼ cup pomegranate molasses + extra for garnishing (see Cook's Note)

Good pinch ground cardamom

Small pinch of freshly ground black pepper

1 cup pomegranate seeds/arils

2 cups plain full-fat greek yogurt

1 cup granola of your choice

½ cup crushed roasted pistachios

1. Using a vegetable peeler, remove 4 strips of orange peel. Then juice the orange and reserve ¼ cup (you can drink the rest!).

2. Combine orange juice, orange peel, honey, pomegranate molasses, ground cardamom, and pepper in a small saucepan. Set over medium heat, and simmer for 2 minutes to bring all the flavors together. Remove from heat, pull out orange peels, and allow to cool for 5 minutes.

3. Pour pomegranate seeds into a small bowl. Pour infused honey syrup over the pomegranate seeds and stir to combine.

4. In a medium bowl, whisk yogurt until smooth.

5. Assemble parfaits: Spoon ½ cup yogurt into the bottom of a glass. Add ¼ cup granola. Add pomegranate relish. Garnish with pistachios. Serve!

CHAPTER 10

When You Need Guidance

It was a grey snowed-in day in the North Carolina mountains. The last day of the year, I'd stumbled upon a copy of *My Utmost for His Highest* by Oswald Chambers in my in-laws' cabin. I turned to the last entry, for December 31, and these final words echoed in my confused heart: "Step out into the invincible future with Him."

But in which direction? I was sick of treading water. I'd been waiting on God to show me where to step next, how to exit the wilderness of nothingness. But He seemed quiet. Oh for a theologically sound magic 8-ball to help me figure out which way to go! I stared out the window, pleading with God to show me this invincible future that Oswald Chambers talked about. And just then I felt a voice press on my heart: "Pick something. Anything. And I will bless it."

God loves to guide us. How can a good father not? I think about my own daughters. When they ask me for wisdom, it brings me so much joy because, selfishly, it shows me that they value my judgment! Similarly, asking for God's guidance is actually a form of worship; we exalt His infinite and wise nature when we reach our hands up to heaven and say, Help!

The LORD directs the steps of the godly. He delights in every detail of their lives. Though they stumble, they will never fall, for the LORD holds them by the hand.
PSALM 37:23-24 NLT

Oh my friend, what a joy to know that every moment of our lives has been plotted out by the Creator, the epitome of goodness and wisdom, the all-knowing, all-powerful, present-everywhere-at-the-same-time God! Yes, even the painful parts the enemy meant for evil, our Father uses for good. This is our privilege as ones who have surrendered our lives to Christ. As C. H. Spurgeon puts it, "Our every step is the subject of divine decree." What is true of our past is true of our present and our future. He goes before us and makes the rough places smooth. He covers our rear guard. He holds our hand as we walk, day by day, step by step.

Sometimes I hold this subconscious belief that God carries me out of some kind of reluctant obligation, that He grumpily harrumphs when I ask Him for help. But Psalm 37:23-24 tells us the opposite. God delights in every detail of our lives. To be delighted is to experience extreme satisfaction and joy, to take great pleasure in something. Can you imagine that for a moment? God plans the twists and turns out of our lives, not out of some self-obsessed megalomania but out of pure joy and love for us.

While it's easy to look within for the solutions to our problems, God urges us to come to Him. Jesus echoes David's sentiments in this psalm when He said: "Ask, and it will be given to you" (Matthew 7:7 ESV).

In fact, you can actually read that line as "keep asking." Keep asking, my friend. Keep knocking, keep seeking. Because, as Jesus goes on to say, our Father is a good parent who longs to "give what is good to those who ask Him!"

What happens when we've asked for guidance but we've received silence? Jesus encourages us to ask with a believing heart. This is the walking-on-water part of asking: acting as if God is already working on the answer. We must make a decision to believe that God has answered the prayer, but that we just haven't seen it manifest yet. What does that look like? Well, think of it this way.

My girls love Pokemon Go. My oldest will often ask my husband when we're out in the world, "Can we check if there are any Pokemon around"? She opens up the app on his phone and looks at the world through the eyes of the game, where suddenly wild animated characters lurk behind every corner. With a gasp of excitement, she launches a poke-ball at the creature, capturing it for her arsenal. What is invisible to my naked eye is a field of possibility to her. In the same way, when we've asked God for guidance, we must look at the world around us through His filter. What seems impossible to us is but a snap of the heavenly finger.

> We honor Him when we reach our hands up to heaven and say, Help!

And lastly, know that His guidance will often fly in the face of what is comfortable for us. So often He has directed me to do things that feel impossible, dangerous, countercultural. Often, when facing a few pathways, I know deep down which one He wants me to follow: the one where I foresee myself stumbling, skinning my knee, or much, much worse. Dear heart, when we ask for guidance, let's check our hearts: Are we asking for the thumbs-up to skirt the road chock-full of stumbles? David says, "Though they stumble, they will never fall." Failure, difficulty, and trouble often litter the "right" path. We cannot escape hardship. And indeed, it can often feel like choosing the right path is choosing the rough path. When we show up at heaven's door, I see us covered in bruises and Band-Aids, and yet victorious, having lived the truth of the old Japanese proverb, "Fall down seven times, get up eight."

Ours is not the easy road. It is narrow, littered with stumbling blocks. And yet, we don't walk this road alone. Our Father delights in walking alongside us, whispering directions to us like some sort of GPS for our lives. Sometimes He has concrete directions for us. Sometimes He's willing to bless whatever direction we choose. But one thing is constant: when we ask God directions, our prayers are safe in His all-knowing hands. So, just as my daughter sees a whole new world when she looks at it through the app on her father's phone, perhaps we must look at our lives similarly. If we have asked, He is answering.

> ## What seems impossible to us is but a snap of the heavenly finger.

So, just as my daughter sees a whole new world when she looks through the app on her father's phone, perhaps we must look at our lives similarly. Let's look back to look forward. Let's look at the world through the filter of one who has tasted His goodness before, as one who knows that our steps are ordered and established by the source of all wisdom in creation. Let's walk knowing that our Father takes great joy and satisfaction in holding our hands, that He guards our rear, clearing off the road before us. Let's listen for His voice whispering words of encouragement as we stomp toward victory.

Our future is invincible, darling one, not because we are, but because He is.

Sorrow may bring us to the earth, and death may bring us to the grave, but lower we cannot sink, and out of the lowest of all we shall arise to the highest of all.

C. H. SPURGEON

I chose a donut recipe here because I'd like you to peer at the world around you through it! There's something child-like about that action that reminds me that while I don't see the whole story, I am on a first-name basis with its Author. And He's right next to me, guiding me through every twist and turn.

Matcha Donuts

MAKES 12 SERVINGS | **TOTAL TIME:** 2 HOURS 40 MINUTES | **ACTIVE TIME:** 40 MINUTES

4¼ cups (510g) all purpose flour

¼ cup (64g) granulated sugar

2 teaspoons (6g or 1 packet) instant or rapid-rise yeast

1¼ cups whole milk

2 large eggs

2 teaspoons vanilla extract

1¼ teaspoon (10g) fine sea salt

8 tablespoons (1 stick) unsalted butter, melted and cooled

2 quarts neutral oil (such as vegetable or canola) for frying

Matcha glaze:

1 cup (5 ounces) confectioner's sugar

1½ teaspoons matcha powder

Pinch of fine sea salt

3 tablespoons hot water

Matcha sugar topping:

½ cup (113g) granulated sugar

1½ teaspoons matcha powder

Pinch of fine sea salt

1. Stir flour, sugar, and yeast together in the bowl of your stand mixer. Add milk, eggs, vanilla extract, salt, and butter, mixing with a rubber spatula until well combined.

2. Attach the dough hook, and mix on medium-low speed until a ball forms, 1 to 2 minutes. Add more flour, 2 tablespoons at a time, if the dough is too sticky.

3. Grease a large bowl with oil. Pop the dough into this bowl, cover with plastic wrap or a damp cloth, and allow to sit at room temperature for 1 hour or until it has doubled in size. (If your counter tends to run cold, fold a kitchen towel and place it between your bowl and your counter so the dough doesn't get cold.)

4. Turn dough out onto a floured surface. Divide into 12 even portions and roll into balls. Flatten one and pinch through the center with your thumb and forefinger, then gently form a 3-inch ring.

5. Place doughnuts on 2 floured sheet pans, leaving a generous amount of room between them. Allow to rise in a warm place for 45 minutes.

6. About 20 minutes before donuts are done rising, warm oil in a heavy bottomed pot or Dutch oven over medium-low heat to 375 degrees

Fahrenheit. Set a wire rack in another sheet pan, and line it with a double layer of paper towels.

7. Carefully add doughnuts to the hot oil, either using your fingers or a metal spatula. You should be able to cook 3 to 4 at a time. Fry until bottoms are deep golden brown, about 45 seconds. Use a spider skimmer or a slotted spoon to flip them over. Cook until they're deep golden brown all over. Transfer doughnuts to prepared rack to cool.

8. Matcha frosting: whisk together sugar, matcha and salt, then add hot water. Whisk until smooth.

9. Matcha sugar: whisk together sugar and matcha powder

10. Toss half of the still-warm donuts in the matcha sugar. Set aside.

11. Dip the tops of the remaining doughnuts in the matcha glaze. Allow frosting to set up, about 20 minutes.

12. Serve!

When You Need Sustenance

CHAPTER 11

When You Need to Be Sustained

The *BFG* by Roald Dahl begins with a bit of a nightmare. A big, scary giant (we don't yet know he's big and friendly) kidnaps a little girl named Sophie. In an effort to save her from a tribe of children-eating (*not* friendly and *even* bigger) giants, the BFG tucks her into the hollows of one of his massive ears, then runs home, far away from the city. Sophie is amazed, watching the world from a giant's eye view; the towering buildings of her hometown look like Legos. The wind zips through her hair as she traverses a distance impossible to cross in her own strength.

He never lets go.

Quite often, the burdens of life weigh heavy on my shoulders. I don't have the strength, energy, or willingness to run the race set before me. Turning my eyes to heaven, with tears at their corners, I look for some glimpse of His great, warm ear carrying me across the rough, craggy terrain. "Where are You?" I cry.

> *Listen to me . . . I've been carrying you on my back from the day you were born, and I'll keep on carrying you when you're old. I'll be there, bearing you when you're old and gray. I've done it and will keep on doing it, carrying you on my back, saving you.*
> ISAIAH 46:3-4 THE MESSAGE

Oh. There You are, God.

The holy Scriptures echo this message over and over. He created us—He knows our capacity or lack thereof. And so He carries us from the womb to the tomb and every moment in between. He never lets go.

So what do we do when we feel exhausted and defeated? When we need to feel some of that sustenance, or nourishment, in order to keep going?

> *Cast your burden upon the LORD and He will sustain you;*
> *He will never allow the righteous to be shaken.*
> PSALM 55:22 NASB

I shake my head vigorously when someone says, "God doesn't give us more than we can handle." No, dear heart. God often gives us precisely more than we can handle. Look at almost every prophet, leader, hero, and heroine in the Bible—they were given way more than they could handle, all so they could be stunning witnesses to the strength, mercy, and glory of God. In our weakness, He is strong, right?

Another thing to consider is that your exhaustion might be the result of your carrying a burden that wasn't meant to sit solely on your shoulders. Jesus doesn't call the self-sufficient and strong. He calls the weary, the downtrodden, and the broken-hearted! If that's you, then I have good news: Jesus wants to lift that burden off your shoulders and replace it with His because, by comparison, fastening ourselves to Him is easy, and His burden is light (Matthew 11:30).

> In our weakness, He is strong.

So cast that burden off, my friend! The word cast here depicts an energetic flinging off, the way you'd happily drop a heavy backpack after carrying it through an airport on a travel day. Drop it, my friend! Let it emit a loud thud as it hits the floor. It's not for you to carry on your own! Commit it to His care. Surrender it to His hands.

Surrender is the key to being sustained.

Lastly, a warning. Be careful that you're not seeking sustenance from anyone or anything else but God, first and foremost. When we're on our last legs, it's so tempting to take help offered from places we'd never accept at the beginning of the race. Peter, the rock of the church, paints an ominous picture of this, after he mirrors that very verse from Psalms:

> *Cast all your anxiety on Him because He cares for you. Be*
> *alert and of sober mind. Your enemy the devil prowls around*
> *like a roaring lion looking for someone to devour.*
> I PETER 5:7-8 NIV

Predators always pounce when their prey is at their most exhausted. The enemy of our souls is no different. When we want to give up, that's when he enters with confusion, lies, and division. Stay alert, friend, and whisper your woes into His almighty ear. Try to see your life, the one He gave you, from His perspective. Don't shoulder it on your own. Instead, hand it back to Him, crouch in the hollows, and watch as He carries you across valleys and peaks that seemed insurmountable! This is hard, yes. So hard. But you aren't meant to carry this burden alone. He's had you from your mother's womb, and He'll carry you until you're gray and even beyond! And one day, we'll see each other at the joyful feast Jesus has been preparing for us, and we'll throw our arms around each other as we sing these words from "Amazing Grace" with a deep, weary yet grateful understanding, having run the race set before us: "Through many dangers, toils, and snares, I have already come! 'Tis grace hath brought me safe thus far, and grace shall lead me home."

Surrender it to His hands.

I leave you with a recipe that always feels like comfort and sustenance: creamy Dal Makhani (Creamy North Indian Lentils). I love it with the everyday griddled flatbread I grew up with, chapati. But you can also eat it with some whole wheat tortillas. There's something about the simplicity of luxurious lentils wrapped up in a piece of flatbread that comforts me, both in their preparation and in their consumption. I pray it will sustain you too.

Dal Makhani
(Creamy North Indian Lentils)

MAKES 4 TO 6 SERVINGS | **TOTAL TIME:** 40 MINUTES | **ACTIVE TIME:** 15 MINUTES

1 medium yellow onion, diced

1 large clove garlic, finely chopped

1-inch thumb ginger, finely chopped

2 tablespoons ghee

1 tablespoon avocado oil

3 to 4 bay leaves

2 dried red chilis

1 cinnamon stick

1 teaspoon cumin seeds

1 8-ounce can tomato sauce

1 teaspoon garam masala

¾ teaspoon paprika

½ teaspoon ground cumin

1 15-ounce can lentils

1 15-ounce can red kidney beans

¼ cup heavy cream or coconut cream

2 teaspoons dried fenugreek leaves, crumbled between your fingers

Kosher salt

1. Drop onions into a mini food processor and process until finely chopped. Add garlic and ginger, and process again until somewhere between finely minced and a coarse paste.

2. Set a large Dutch oven over medium heat, add ghee, avocado oil, bay leaves, red chilis, cinnamon stick and cumin seeds. Once the whole spices start sizzling, add the onion mixture. Season with a pinch of salt, and cook, stirring often, until onions are lightly golden and smell sweet, about 8 to 10 minutes.

3. Stir in tomato sauce, garam masala, paprika, and ground cumin. Saute until most of the liquid has evaporated and mixture deepens in color, 3 to 4 minutes.

4. Add lentils, beans, and ½ teaspoon kosher salt. Toss to coat with the masala (spice mixture in the pot) and cook, stirring often, about 30 seconds.

5. Now add hot water and stir well. Raise heat to high, bring to a boil, then reduce heat so pot is at a gentle simmer. Cook uncovered for 20 to 25 minutes until curry thickens, stirring every now and then.

6. Pull out bay leaves, chilis and cinnamon stick.

7. Rub dried fenugreek leaves between palms to turn them into a powder, and stir into the curry. Turn off the heat, and stir in the cream. Taste and add more salt if necessary. Serve with rice, chapatis, or warm whole wheat tortillas.

CHAPTER 12

When You Need to Be Filled

Whenever we're on a road trip, my husband makes fun of the way my shoulders tense up whenever I notice the gas indicator descend past the halfway mark. I'm petrified of running out of gas, mostly because it happened to us once, and while I won't go into the story here for fear of recording it for all of human history, I'm just going to say that Bren now knows that I'm right.

And yet, while I won't let myself run on empty in my car, I frequently run on empty myself.

Juggling myriad identities—wife, mother, daughter, sister, friend, chef, TV personality, social media person (I can't bring myself to use the word influencer!), speaker, author, producer—is dizzying. Often I'll find myself panting, exhausted in every sense of the word. I'll reach for creature comforts like a pedicure, a pint of ice cream, or a bath, and while they soothe for a little while, I always end up in the same position of fatigue, hopelessness, and discontent. At that point, even the tried and true verses highlighted in my Bible ring hollow, and worship music sounds trite and overly simplistic. Am I the only one?

> The Holy Spirit is a supernatural reboot that supercharges our lives for His glory.

At that point, I know I'm in trouble and in need of some serious intervention. The E has been flickering for way too long on my dashboard. I need a fresh filling of the Holy Spirit.

What does that mean? Well, every person who chooses to follow Jesus is sealed with a deposit of the Holy Spirit. That never changes. But the experience of being filled with the Holy Spirit happens (hopefully) many times in our lives. It's our fuel, a recharge from heaven, a supernatural reboot that supercharges our lives for His glory. The Holy Spirit pulls on our reins, telling us when and where to go and not go. To be filled with the Holy Spirit means that we allow Him to occupy every nook and cranny of our lives, so that He can move us to be fruitful in His kingdom.

Paul charges us to "be filled with the Holy Spirit" (Ephesians 5:18 NLT) and compares it to the feeling of being intoxicated by wine, but I think you could also compare it to being intoxicated by a person! It takes control over your body and your mind. I think about my very first boyfriend—I couldn't stop thinking about him all day long! He was the first thought when I woke up and the last before I went to bed. That's how I'm supposed to feel about God, possibly multiplied by about one thousand. Sound impossible? Not with the Holy Spirit. I know I'm not at that point right now, friend, so know that I'm speaking to myself just as much as I'm speaking to you. You and I need to refuel.

Being filled with the Holy Spirit means we get the benefit of experiencing the many-segmented fruit of the Spirit (love, joy, peace, patience, kindness, goodness, faithfulness, gentleness, and self-control).

> The Holy Spirit lets the Light in and helps us to see God's goodness.

Being filled with the Holy Spirit leads to praise and worship. It breaks through the hard shell that builds around our hearts as we crawl through the difficulties of life. It lets the Light in and helps us to see God's goodness no matter our circumstances. In that way, our worship is intoxicating to those around us who may need a refilling themselves! It edifies our neighbor, and it illuminates the darkness. Glory, glory.

And so, if we're running on empty, if we're parched for His living water, here's a few things we can do to invite Him to fill our well. First, examine your heart. The Spirit cannot fill what is not empty. He cannot fill a seat that's already occupied. Are we totally surrendered to Him? Or are there areas of our lives where we're still in the driver's seat, instead of riding shotgun?

Second, we can "grieve the Holy Spirit" (Ephesians 4:30 ESV) and inhibit His direction and power in our lives. Are there any practices or beliefs in our lives that might be causing the Holy Spirit to grieve over us? Are we willing to turn away from them?

Finally, let's ask Him to fill us back up. God is a generous and good Father. When we ask for those things that line up with His will, He is happy to give and give in droves! So, would you pray with me?

PRAY WITH ME

Father, hear our prayer. Thank You for lighting up the E sign on our dashboard! Thank You for inviting us back to the well to be filled up. Thank You for Your kind heart that is always seeking our good. Your heart is such a thing of beauty and sweetness,

God. I long for Your living water to quench my parched heart. I've been running on empty and I need You. I repent of every choice I've made that has grieved the Holy Spirit. Please fill me with Your Holy Spirit! I want to want You. I want to be intoxicated by You, for Your glory, for my satisfaction, and for the good of all those around me.

Thank You, Lord, for calling me back to the well. You are such a good, good God. My soul exalts You, O Lord. Amen.

God is a generous and good Father.

There are few things in the culinary world that feel as nourishing as a bowl of soup, and a noodle soup perhaps most of all! Here's my favorite version, Laksa, which you'll find all over Southeast Asia, but I first encountered it in Singapore. This soup fires on all cylinders, enchanting the eyes with that bright golden broth and intoxicating the nasal passages with the aromas of ginger, turmeric, and coriander. And yet it's just a glimmer of the way the Lord intends to fill us with every good thing.

Laksa: Singaporean Coconut Noodle Soup

MAKES 6 SERVINGS | **TOTAL TIME:** 1 HOUR 20 MINUTES | **ACTIVE TIME:** 30 MINUTES

Cook's Note: Yes, this is a lot of stuff. If you'd like to skip making the curry paste from scratch, you can substitute with a few tablespoons of Thai red curry paste and 2 teaspoons of curry powder!

3 small dried red chilis, such as chile d'árbol

2 tablespoons (20g) raw cashews

5 large shallots (210g), coarsely chopped (about 1 cup)

5 large garlic cloves

2-inch piece ginger (20g), peeled and chopped

1 stalk lemongrass, root end and woody husk removed, finely chopped, bottom 8-inches only

2 Fresno chilis (optional)

2 teaspoons ground coriander or coriander seeds

1 teaspoon ground turmeric

1 teaspoon sweet paprika

1 bunch fresh cilantro, leaves and soft stems divided

6 tablespoons peanut, coconut, or avocado oil, divided

1 pound large shell-on shrimp, peels removed but not discarded

4 cups chicken stock

1½ tablespoons light brown sugar

1½ tablespoon fish sauce, divided, plus more as needed (recommended: Red Boat)

1 14.5-ounce can full-fat coconut milk

2 teaspoons lime zest (from 1 lime)

1 tablespoon lime juice (from ½ lime)

1 pound flat rice noodles, such as Pad Thai noodles

Lime wedges, bean sprouts, fried shallots, and chili garlic sauce for serving

1. Boil kettle of water. Soak red chilis and cashews in hot water for 20 minutes. Drain. Remove seeds from chilis if you prefer less heat.

2. Laksa paste: Drop shallots, garlic, ginger, lemongrass, ground coriander, turmeric, paprika, cilantro stems, drained red chilis and cashews, and 2 tablespoons oil into a blender and process until a smooth paste forms.

3. Pour ¼ cup oil into a large Dutch oven and heat over medium high until it starts to smoke. Add the shrimp shells along with a pinch of salt. Cook, stirring every now and then, until shells turn chestnut brown, 3 to 4 minutes.

4. Now scoop out paste from blender into the pot. Stir constantly, making sure to coat the shrimp shells in the laksa paste, and cook about 2 minutes, until paste starts to thicken.

5. Pour 2 cups of water into the blender jar. Put the lid back on and give it a shake to capture any remaining laksa paste. Pour that into the pot along with chicken stock and brown sugar. Bring to boil, turn down to simmer, cover, and cook for 30 minutes.

6. Meanwhile, toss shrimp with 1 tablespoon fish sauce. Set in the fridge to marinate.

7. Separately, bring a large saucepan of water to a boil. Turn the heat off. Add the noodles, and allow to sit for 10 minutes, until tender but still chewy. Drain and rinse in cool water. Divide noodles between bowls.

8. Strain the soup broth through a fine strainer set over a large heat-safe bowl, pressing down on the shells to extract as much flavor as possible. Pour the broth back into the pot and discard the solids. Add coconut milk and fish sauce. Turn heat to medium high and bring soup back to a simmer.

9. Remove shrimp from the refrigerator and drop into the simmering soup. Cook about 2 minutes, until tender.

10. Turn the heat off. Finish the soup with lime juice, lime zest, and more fish sauce if needed. Serve broth and shrimp over noodles, accompanied by fresh beans sprouts, cilantro leaves, chili garlic sauce, and fried shallots.

CHAPTER 13

When You Need Encouragement

I pulled on the slightly too-tight black velvet maxi dress we'd just found at a thrift store in Palm Desert, California, and looked at myself disapprovingly in the mirror. I was getting ready for a "Meet the Chefs" party at a food festival there, and having looked at the list of high-powered chefs in attendance, imposter syndrome kicked into high gear. Who was I to be listed alongside these people? Would the organizers regret their decision to include me when they saw that the guests didn't know me or, if they did, didn't care? I girded myself with the two weapons I always reach for when I feel this way—big dangly earrings and red lipstick—and stepped out of the bathroom.

"Oh wow, Mama!" my two wee daughters cried.

"Yeah?" I said. "Look okay? I'm feeling a bit nervous, girls."

"Oh, Mama. You look like a *queen*! You go there and remember that!"

> To encourage someone is to speak courage into their bones.

There's something about children encouraging you that pierces through every self-deprecating argument you'd raise if an adult tried to do the same. Their sweet, wide-open faces, the way they put their hands on their hips and raised a sassy finger when they said "remember that!". . . Even if I didn't believe that I was a queen, I believed that they believed I looked like one, and I didn't want to let them down. So I smiled, raised my chin a little higher, and walked out of the hotel room determined to go do my job to the best of my ability, whether people were happy to see me or not.

To encourage someone is to speak courage into their bones; it stokes the glimmering embers of fortitude and valor in their heart of hearts. It reminds them of who they are, and in the case of you and me, dearest brethren in Christ, it reminds us of Whose they are.

"Blessed be the God and Father of our Lord
Jesus Christ, the Father of compassions,
and God of all encouragement."
II CORINTHIANS 1:3 DARBY

There are so many names for God in the Old Testament: El Shaddai (the Almighty), Jehovah Jireh (the Lord will provide), and possibly the most tongue-twisting one of all: Jehovah Mekoddishkem (the Lord who sanctifies you)!

And yet here, Paul gives God a name that reveals His softer, more intimate side: God of all encouragement. It's His very nature, friend, to pick us up when we're feeling faint. While we may think of Scripture as a list of rules and regulations, the reality is that the Bible is mostly a book of encouragements and reminders of who God is, and who we are in relation to Him. I've heard it said that there's a "do not fear" verse for nearly every day of the year because He knows what fearful creatures we are, but there's also thousands of other verses encouraging us in other ways!

Such things were written in the Scriptures long ago to teach
us. And the Scriptures give us hope and encouragement as
we wait patiently for God's promises to be fulfilled.
ROMANS 15:4 NLT

If we are seeking encouragement, our first stop on our own personal revival tour should be the Bible. Its author is the God of encouragement, after all. Scripture is filled with stories of God's people, seeking Him with fear and trembling, because without Him, they didn't think they could complete the task He'd set before them. Every single character in the Bible (apart from Jesus) is fallible, just like us: Moses had a temper problem and a speech impediment; David was a teenager with a lust problem; Esther was fearful and, at least at first, didn't seem to have much of a relationship with God.

> Take courage! Our future is secure in Him.

And yet they all persevered to some version of victory, because God encouraged them and stood by them.

When we crack open our Bibles to read these stories of the heroes of yore, they encourage us in the here and now and give us hope for the future. For what is despair but a fear of what the future holds? Take courage! Our future is secure in Him.

Scripture encourages us by recording His promises in black and white. It's one thing to make a promise in word alone. But it's quite another to put it in writing. You can bank on the written record, my love. So here are some of my favorite promises.

Look them up, and write them out. I think there's great power in writing verses down. It slows us down and helps us to absorb every word into the marrow of our bones. And as Proverbs teaches, "Gracious words are . . . healing to the bones" (Proverbs 16:24 NIV)!

God knows who I am and cares about every little thing about me. Psalm 139:1-6

God has a plan for my life, because I love Him. I Corinthians 2:9

God is invested in me. Psalm 32:8

God is with me wherever I go so there is no reason to fear. Joshua 1:9

God will help me overcome trouble. John 16:33

God is holding me up even when I feel like I'm falling. Isaiah 41:10

God is giving me peace, even now. Isaiah 26:3

God will provide for me. Philippians 4:19

God will protect me. Psalm 84:11

> ## It's His love, along with His promises, that causes the fire to ignite!

Let these promises serve as mighty logs you can throw on the dying embers of courage in your heart, beloved. Think of His love as the bellows blowing fresh oxygen over the hearth. It's His love, along with His promises, that causes the fire to ignite! There's nothing that can separate us from His love, and if that's true, then there's nothing that can separate us from His promises. Be encouraged, my courageous friend.

There is such love and grace in the heart of God [that] if you understood the length and breadth and height and depth of it, you would never be discouraged.

JONATHAN EDWARDS

I've always adored the flavors of food cooked over an open flame. Perhaps it's that the bitterness of a charred exterior more dramatically brings out the sweetness of what lies beneath. As you stare at the blue flames licking at the thin peel of bell peppers and the dates, remember that His love is both the oxygen and the fuel that lights us up.

Charred Date and Halloumi Salad with Bells and Olives

MAKES 4 SERVINGS | **TOTAL TIME**: 35 MINUTES | **ACTIVE TIME**: 25 MINUTES

4 sweet bell peppers (red and yellow)

5 California dates, pitted

Small handful olives, pitted (black and green)

Small handful toasted almonds, chopped

Handful parsley leaves

Splash sherry vinegar

Juice of a quarter lemon

Glug of extra virgin olive

Salt and freshly ground black pepper

1 block halloumi, patted dry and sliced into ½-inch thick rectangles

1 to 2 bamboo skewers, soaked in water for 20 minutes

1. Place bell peppers over an open flame on your stove. Rotate and cook until evenly blackened. Remove to a large bowl and immediately cover with plastic wrap. Let sit 5 to 10 minutes. Remove plastic wrap and peel charred skin. Discard. Now slice peppers thinly, removing stem and core. Place in serving bowl.

2. While peppers are steaming, thread pitted California dates on a bamboo skewer. Brush with a little oil and then roast over an open flame until charred in places. Place in the fridge to cool for 10 minutes. Remove from skewer then slice and add to pepper.

3. Now add olives, almonds, and parsley. Dress with a splash of sherry vinegar, a squeeze of lemon, and a good glug of olive oil. Season with salt and freshly ground black pepper. Toss to combine, taste for seasoning.

4. Set a large nonstick skillet over medium to medium-high heat, add a glug of olive oil, and heat until shimmering. Place halloumi slices in skillet and cook until golden brown, about 3 to 4 minutes. Flip and cook other side similarly. Remove and serve immediately with date salad.

CHAPTER 14

When You Need a Sure Thing

I've always hated feeling dizzy. As a child, merry-go-rounds and tea-cup rides were my nemeses. When I got to college, my nemesis reappeared in the form of "the spins," the nasty aftermath of mixing beer and wine. My father-in-law taught me an antidote: Lie down on the couch, but keep one foot on the floor. Even though my mind told me the world was whirling like a dervish, the solid, unchanging wood beneath my feet reminded me of the truth that nothing was moving.

(Side note: I'm fully aware that this isn't the typical metaphor you'd use in a devotional, my friend. But I'm willing to bet that most of us have been there!)

Jesus Christ is the same yesterday, today and forever.
HEBREWS 13:8

The very nature of our lives is change. We enter the world with smooth skin and bald heads, and we exit with wrinkles and a silver crown. Even now as I type, my body is aging. And yet, Christ is at once as ancient as time and as fresh as a newborn in the manger.

> We are always changing. He is always staying the same.

We are always changing. He is always staying the same.

As I write this, enormous changes challenge my sure footing: politics, philosophy, technology, economies, wars, pandemics, crises within and without . . . Wow, does it feel overwhelming right now. What once felt like steady ground feels like a jello trampoline. It all feels so much bigger than me. And yet, whether it's Egypt, Babylon, Rome, or even the ding-dang serpent in the Garden, nothing has been able to stamp out Jehovah, amen?

Nothing and no one can extinguish Him. Death tried. And it lost. Hallelujah!

Do you see how we are a dizzying vortex of change? We are constantly changing beings, living in a world that constantly changes. To find steady ground, we must look outside of ourselves and outside of this world, and plant our feet on the only unchanging One in existence: Jesus. His steady reliability is evident in something as simple as the way He draws the sun into the morning sky every. single. day. We set our clocks to His faithfulness! No one else can ease our furrowed brow like He can.

> Nothing and no one can extinguish Him. Death tried. And it lost. Hallelujah!

Where we tire, He never grows weary.

Where we give in to temptation, He holds the line and shames temptation back to the darkness.

Where we're motivated by self-preservation, He's motivated by self-sacrifice.

And where we are thrown about by the storms, He commands them to "be still."

What a relief, and what a source of hope that no matter how wildly instability rages in our lives, no matter how it shivers the timbers of our sailboat, the dry, steady shore is just a prayer away.

"As the Father loves me, so have I loved you," He whispers to us. Let's keep our ears tuned to His whisper, darlin'. Sometimes the challenges in our lives are the result of the world's brokenness. Sometimes they're from the devil himself. Still other times, they're the result of God's discipline in our lives. Through all these circumstances, the Lord's love for us never changes. We may feel like He's distant, like He has withdrawn from us. But more than likely, we're the ones who have changed. Think of the phases of the moon; she appears to change shape, but in actuality she's the same! We're the ones who have moved.

When I worked at CNN, I covered a landslide in an affluent area of Southern California. Magnificent mansions tumbled into the ravines, their owners fleeing with just the shirts on their backs. It was hard to believe that such sturdy-looking houses could fall away like cardboard. Let's not do the same thing, dear heart. Where have we built our homes? Are our hopes and dreams built on the shifting sands of this world? Or are they built on the bedrock of Christ? Because if it's the former, I can tell you from experience, it takes just one heavy rain to wash the floor out from under you. When we're deeply rooted in Christ, we become like Paul:

I have learned the secret of living in every situation, whether it is with a full stomach or empty, with plenty or little. For I can do everything through Christ, who gives me strength.
PHILIPPIANS 4:12-13 (NLT)

So often it feels like life is random, mercurial, chaotic, and out of control. And yet it is in control. And the One at the helm is worthy of the position. Jesus is not only wise, but He is good, righteous, and faithful. He's the man for the job. And so, when life throws you a curveball that leaves you spinning ... dizzy ... lie back on Him and plant your foot down on the firm foundation that is Jesus. Remind yourself that even though it feels like everything is out of control, everything is firmly in His hands. Always has been. Always will be.

Where we tire, He never grows weary.

Question: As you make one of the oldest recipes in the world, the meat pie (scratched into Mesopotamian tablets from the 1700s!), consider a characteristic of Jesus' nature that is the most comfort to you when you're dizzied by the challenges in your life. Is it His patience? His power? His faithfulness? Write a prayer to Him, thanking Him for being exactly what you need right now. And see if you can hear Him say back to you, "Just as the Father loved me, so have I loved you!"

Curry Puffs

MAKES 16 CURRY PUFFS | TOTAL TIME: 1 HOUR 50 MINUTES | ACTIVE TIME: 1 HOUR

1 tablespoon whole coriander seeds

¼ cup avocado oil

3 medium bay leaves

2 teaspoons caraway or cumin seeds

1 large yellow onion, finely chopped (about 2 cups)

Kosher salt and freshly ground black pepper

1 pound ground chicken

2 teaspoons curry powder

½ cup coconut cream

2 teaspoons cornstarch

⅔ cup minced cilantro leaves and soft stems

17.3 ounce box frozen puff pastry, thawed overnight in the fridge (recommended: Pepperidge Farm)

1 large egg, lightly beaten

1. Tip whole coriander seeds into a large heavy-bottomed skillet. Set over medium heat, and cook, shaking the pan frequently until seeds deepen in color and are fragrant. Pour into a mortar and pestle, and bash until you get a coarse powder (alternatively, pour onto your chopping board and use a heavy pan).

2. Warm avocado oil in same large skillet over medium heat until shimmering. Add bay leaves and whole caraway seeds. Cook about 20 to 30 seconds, until they're dancing around the pan and fragrant. Now add the onions, season with salt and cook until softened and translucent, about 5 minutes.

3. Push the onion mix to the side of the pan and add the ground chicken to the center of the pan and season with salt.

Allow to cook for 4 to 5 minutes, until fully cooked through. Once cooked, mix everything in the pan together.

4. Season with freshly ground black pepper and sprinkle with curry powder. Cook another 30 to 45 seconds, stirring frequently to avoid burning the spices.

5. Pour in coconut cream and ¼ cup water. Stir and cook until most of the water is evaporated; the mixture should be thick and creamy. Taste for seasoning, then stir in cornstarch.

6. Take the skillet off the heat. Add the cilantro and then pour the mixture onto a sheet pan to cool off, about 20 minutes.

7. Preheat oven to 400 degrees Fahrenheit. Line a sheet pan with parchment paper.

8. Lightly flour your counter. Pull out one sheet of puff pastry, and using a rolling pin, roll to double its size (e.g., if it's a 9-inch square, roll to a 18-inch square)

9. Using a 4½-inch bowl, cut out circles from the dough. You can re-roll the scraps too.

10. Paint a ring of egg wash around the perimeter of each circle using a pastry brush. Place 2 tablespoons of the cooled filling in the center of each circle. Fold the pastry over to create a semi-circle, then crimp the edges together by pressing down the tines of a fork into them to create a frilly edge. Place on prepared sheet pan.

11. Brush each curry puff evenly with egg wash, making sure to gild the frilly edge too. Pop into the oven and bake for 10 to 15 minutes, until golden brown. Cool for 5 minutes before serving.

CHAPTER 15

When You Need Courage

*Yea, though I walk through the valley of the shadow of death, I will fear
no evil; for You are with me; Your rod and Your staff, they comfort me.*
PSALM 23:4 NKJV

I was watching a famous South Indian movie this week, *RRR*. We first meet one of the heroes in the middle of the jungle. He pours the blood of an unknown animal over his head. Within seconds, he hears the snarl of a wolf who gives chase. Our hero takes off, heading toward a trap he'd set just for the wolf. Unfortunately for our hero, he happens to run past an even fiercer predator: a tiger. It finds his augmented scent irresistible and gives chase. Now our hero is trying to outrun not one but two predators! I won't give the ending away (the movie is great!).

But I will say that when I happened to read Psalm 23 the next day, despite having read it probably a thousand times, I saw something I'd never seen before.

> We weren't created to walk through life on our own.

See, just as the hero of *RRR* made himself bait, so too does a shepherd every time he takes his flock out to pasture. Sheep are a tasty, easily hunted morsel for many a predator. And so, to walk alongside a flock of sheep is to walk alongside a tantalizing flock of prey. Should a predator catch one whiff of their scent, should his ears pick up one barmy bleat, the entire flock and the shepherd become a target. Some shepherds will even pen their sheep in overnight and sleep in front of the gate, so that nothing can pass except through him.

To shepherd is to exercise self-sacrifice.

And for what? Sheep are God's creation, so I want to be respectful but . . . let's be honest . . . they're hardly Mensa members! A friend who raises sheep told me that when they travel as a flock, a sheep will blindly follow the sheep in front of it, with nary a glance to the path ahead, which means if that leading sheep walks into a ravine, well, there goes the rest of the flock too.

We are those sheep, beloved. We weren't created to walk through life on our own. We were created to be guided, and if we don't follow the Good Shepherd, then we will follow a bad one. That's just who we are. And so, if you're caught up in fear right now, if you're looking for courage in the face of a scary situation, take heart: feeling fear is a reminder of who we really are! To me, to feel afraid is to acknowledge our own weakness in the face of a bigger, scarier future.

> *For he cannot know that God is his Shepherd unless he*
> *feels in himself that he has the nature of a sheep.*
> CHARLES SPURGEON

Even someone with as much courage, authority, and influence as David, king of Israel, recognized his own "sheepiness." And in fact, I'd like to suggest it was that awareness of his nature that gave him the courage to face down the valley of the shadow of death.

The source of David's courage was his intimacy with the Lord.

Look at the first verse of this psalm. David doesn't say the Lord is *the* shepherd. Or *our* shepherd. No, he says *my* shepherd. There's an intimacy to that title, a sense of there being only two people in that relationship. David belonged to the Lord, and the Lord belonged to him. The Scriptures dub David a man after God's own heart. In fact, David knew the Lord so intimately that he couldn't help but catalog God's very nature in the

Our God is nothing if not courageous.

following lines: provider ("green pastures"), peace-giver ("still waters"), savior ("restores my soul"), teacher ("paths of righteousness"), protector ("valley of the shadow of death"), and so on. David could courageously entrust his future to the Lord because he knew the Lord so well! And so if you're experiencing some fear over your own future, perhaps it's because you don't yet know the Lord that well. Or maybe it's been a while since you spent time with Him, so the memories have grown a little fuzzy. And that's okay! I don't blame you! Why would you feel at peace entrusting your future to a stranger? I believe this is one of the many reasons God calls us to spend time with Him either in prayer or in the Word—so we get to know Him, and in doing so, we deepen our trust in Him.

We become what we worship. And our God is nothing if not courageous. Think of Jesus in the Garden of Gethsemane, acutely aware of the cup set before Him, fearing it in all His humanity, submitting to God in all His divinity. When we deepen our intimacy with Jesus, we become more like Him. Just as He submitted His future to the God He knew and loved so well, so do we submit our future into the hands of our

> **Our courage is rooted in our deep understanding of who holds the future in His hands.**

Good Shepherd. Our courage is rooted not in our own strength or ability, but in a deep understanding of who holds the future in His hands and who we are to Him. While we may not see sheep as valuable, this Shepherd sees us as so precious that it was worth putting His life on the line for us! He put His body in front of us and took the penalty that was meant for us.

Like David, we don't draw our courage from our own rod and staff; we walk through our own valleys of the shadow of death because we trust in the rod and staff of our Shepherd. He already died to save us. What wouldn't He do to protect us now? David, a former shepherd, looked to two pieces of wood—the rod and staff—as a reminder of the Lord's strength and self-sacrificial protection. Dear heart, we have two pieces of wood that serve as an even more powerful reminder of just what lengths our Jesus will go to find us, rescue us, and keep us from harm: the cross. When fear snarls at you like a tiger in the jungle, when the future looks uncertain, look to the cross. We will fear no evil because His rod and staff, that cross, is our constant comfort and hope. Glory, glory.

PRAY WITH ME

Jesus, thank You for being my good, strong, fiercely protective shepherd. Thank You for bringing me to this place, even though it fills my heart with fear. I know that following You means that sometimes, the only way out of the valley is through it. While this whole situation may not work out the way I want, I trust my future to You, Lord. I don't understand it completely, but for some reason, You care about me intimately! Help me to want to know You even more intimately too, so that my courage and faith can grow by Your quiet waters. You are my provider, my protector, and my peace. Thank You, Jesus. Amen.

Jackfruit is a gigantic, rather fearsome looking fruit, covered in spikes, that grows across South and Southeast Asia. As a child, I'd yelp with joy when my dad brought one home from the market; when ripe, its bright yellow fruit tickles the tastebuds with flavors of pineapple, banana, and custard. But it's also useful when it's unripe, because when cooked, its fibrous texture softens, resembling meat. Or, as Bren puts it, "fake prey," which seemed like a funny connection to this devotion given the story I started it with.

Jackfruit Kofta Curry

MAKES 4 TO 5 SERVINGS | TOTAL TIME: 1 HOUR 20 MINUTES | ACTIVE TIME: 1 HOUR

Cook's Note: To make this more realistic for a weeknight, feel free to substitute your favorite jar of curry or simmer sauce for the gravy. You can also airfry the kofta instead of deep frying them. Use ripe fresh tomatoes or canned ones.

1 20-ounce can green/unripe jackfruit, drained

1 small shallot, roughly chopped

¼ cup fresh dill leaves and soft stems

About 10 fresh mint leaves

1 clove garlic, roughly chopped

1 teaspoon ground cumin

2 tablespoons rice flour or all-purpose flour

¼ cup potato flakes (instant mashed potato)

1 large egg, lightly beaten

Peanut or canola oil for frying

Gravy

1 large yellow onion, roughly chopped

4 cloves garlic, finely chopped

½-inch piece ginger, finely chopped

¼ cup avocado oil

1 teaspoon cumin seeds

1 bay leaf

1 teaspoon ground coriander

1 teaspoon ground cumin

1 teaspoon kashmir chili powder (or ½ teaspoon paprika + ½ teaspoon cayenne pepper)

½ teaspoon garam masala

½ tsp turmeric powder

2 medium Roma tomatoes, roughly chopped (see Cook's Note)

¼ cup full-fat coconut milk

Small handful fresh dill to garnish

Small handful mint leaves to garnish

Kosher salt

1. Place drained jackfruit into a small saucepan, and cover with water. Set over high heat and bring to a boil. Turn down to a simmer and cook for about 5 minutes. Strain, discarding water, and set strainer back in empty saucepan for excess water to drain.

2. In a mini food processor, pulse shallot, herbs, garlic, and cumin until fine, but not a paste. Scoop into a large bowl.

3. Pulse half of jackfruit in food processor, until finely chopped. Repeat with remaining half. Add to the shallot mixture in bowl. Sprinkle in rice flour

and potato flakes, followed by egg and 2 teaspoons kosher salt. Stir together with a spatula until well combined.

4. Form small balls, about 1 tablespoon each, and place on a tray. You should get about 24. Refrigerate while you make the curry.

5. Rinse out food processor bowl. Process onion, garlic, and ginger to a smooth paste. Remove to a bowl.

6. Warm oil in a large nonstick wok or skillet over medium-high heat. Add the cumin seeds and bay leaf; cook until sizzling and fragrant, about 30 seconds.

7. Add onion mixture, and sauté until golden brown, 7 to 8 minutes. Meanwhile, puree tomatoes in the food processor and set aside.

8. Add ground coriander, cumin, Kashmir chili, garam masala, and turmeric, and sauté for about a minute until spices are fragrant. Stir in pureed tomato and cook 2 to 3 minutes, until thickened.

9. Stir in coconut milk and 1 cup water, and bring to a boil over high heat. Turn down to low to simmer for 15 minutes, uncovered, until thickened. Use an immersion blender or a regular blender to process curry until smooth.

10. Meanwhile, fill a 10-inch nonstick skillet with a 1-inch depth of peanut or canola oil. Heat over a medium flame to 350 degrees. Carefully drop jackfruit balls into the oil, and check the temperature of the oil. You may need to increase the heat to bring it back to 350 degrees Fahrenheit. Fry until golden brown all over, about 10 minutes. Remove to a paper-towel lined platter.

11. To serve, you can drop the jackfruit kofta into the curry, or serve them separately, to keep the kofta crispy. Garnish with a flurry of dill and mint leaves. Serve with rice or naan.

CHAPTER 16

When You Need Endurance

I stand by the side of the ice bath, vacuuming air through my mouth and then letting it go, slowly heating my body up. I'm going to need it. Wee little whirlpools swirl and babble, but they belie the frosty future that awaits: water kept at or below 40 degrees Fahrenheit. Finally, I'm ready. *I'll go after this breath*, I tell myself. First my feet, then my entire body, followed by my head. And despite having done this for nearly three years now, my first thought is always the same.

Get me out of here!

My head emerges from the polar depths and I let out a loud gasp as the bath begins to wrap its icy tendrils around every limb, joint, toe, hair. My mind screams at me. *Get out! You're going to die!*

> God is not only building our faith but also our endurance.

In response, I begin to breathe in and out through my nose. With every slow, deep breath, I'm forcing my body to accept what my mind knows deep down: Everything is going to be okay. The cold is not comfortable, but exposure therapy heals and strengthens my whole being. Two minutes later, something breaks. The panic bubble pops, and a delicious wave of peace washes over me. I am safe. The cold still nips, but I'm no longer in fear. Now this is just a test of my endurance; how long can I stay?

> *Consider it all joy, my brethren,*
> *when you encounter various trials,*
> *knowing that the testing of your faith*
> *produces endurance.*
> *And let endurance have its perfect result,*
> *so that you may be perfect and complete,*
> *lacking in nothing.*
> JAMES 1:2-4 NASB

Okay, I'm not saying it's for everyone, but one of the reasons I do ice baths is to strengthen my mind to endure the trials either on my plate or on the horizon. What a powerful skill, to keep my mind from hitting the eject button when difficulties arise. And yet sometimes I'm too exhausted, too distressed, too hopeless to breathe my way into endurance. I bet you know that feeling well, my friend. What then?

I love that James doesn't say if trials come our way, but when. Trials are part and parcel of life on earth.

When we're building something, how do we know if it's strong enough without testing it? We bend it, add weight to it, put it under duress so we can find its weak spots. This is how He makes us stronger: by alerting us to our weak spots and joining with us to reinforce them. Is it an easy process? No. But in our trials, God is not only building our faith but also our endurance to wait on Him to do His work in and through us.

And so, if your endurance is fraying around the edges, I'd urge you to imagine you're in the ice bath with me. Let's stop our minds from freaking out! So often, when a trial swipes its talons at me, my instinct is to recoil in fear, then go into solution mode.

But instead, let's stop.

"Consider" as James puts it.

Take a deep, slow breath.

Fire up "We Will Feast in the House of Zion" by Sandra McCracken on your phone.

Hang out here. See what happens at two minutes. Did something break?

When we stop to consider the situation, it's our chance to move from a natural response to a supernatural one. James urges us to respond with joy.

Why joy? Doesn't it seem like a flip response to very real trouble? No, dear heart. Jesus wept. We are free to experience our emotions. We just can't let them rule us. I'm going to borrow from the pastor Tim Keller, who likens Christian joy to a buoy bobbing in the ocean; no matter how big or strong a wave knocks it down, it still pops back up. Joy keeps us upright in the icy waters because we know this isn't the be-all and end-all. Joy is the resilience to resist succumbing to the murky depths. Our joy is not rooted in our situation, but rather in the fact that we are reconciled to Yahweh by Jesus . . . that our Maker moved heaven and earth so we wouldn't perish and be separated from Him forever. Oh rejoice with me, darling one! Glory, glory! We rejoice in the One who said that even though we'd have trials in this world, we are His children now, and so "he who is in you is greater than he who is in the world" (I John 4:4 ESV).

Take a deep, slow breath.

When we choose joy, it helps us zoom out. We stand with Jesus floating above our present. Together we cast our eyes on both the beginning of all things and the end of them. It puts our trial in perspective, which helps us to endure because, compared to our time in eternity, this is nothing. Even if our trial is excruciating, we must hold on, dear heart. When I'm in the ice bath, oh how I ache for the panic bubble to pop so I can experience the peace on the other side! But there's no way to hurry it. Sometimes it takes one minute. Sometimes it takes five. But it always comes. As we patiently wait for this trial to pass, let us remember that Jesus is near. The One who endured the torture and humiliation of the cross stands with us, giving us the strength to persevere. When I look back at times of hardship in my life, I can almost see Him crouched down next to me, one hand rubbing my back, the other helping me get back up.

> Our Maker moved heaven and earth so we wouldn't perish and be separated from Him forever.

He is ever so close to us when our spirits are crushed, my love. Our hearts may scream, "He has abandoned us. We cannot go on." But don't listen. Stop. Take a deep breath. Consider your situation. And choose joy. It will give you the strength to endure.

When I was little, my mum would make me a hot cup of *haldi ka doodh* (what's come to be known as "Golden Milk") whenever I wasn't feeling well. It wouldn't necessarily cure what was ailing me, but it did somehow give me the strength to keep fighting. This is the icy version, a doff of the hat to the ice baths I love so much!

Golden Milk Smoothie Bowls

MAKES 2 SERVINGS | **TOTAL TIME:** 10 MINUTES | **ACTIVE TIME:** 10 MINUTES

¼ cup orange or pineapple juice (or water)

1 cup frozen cubed mango

1 cup plain whole milk yogurt (or nondairy alternative)

1 tablespoon coconut or avocado oil

2 quarter-sized slices fresh ginger

2 tablespoons honey

½ teaspoon ground turmeric

Scant ¼ teaspoon ground cardamom

Big pinch freshly ground black pepper

Pinch of salt

Assorted fruit for toppings

Pepitas or pistachios

Granola

1. Pour orange or pineapple juice (or water) into your blender. Now add frozen mango, yogurt, coconut oil, ginger, honey, ground turmeric, ground cardamom, black pepper, and salt. Put the lid on and blend until smooth.

2. Scoop into two bowls. Adorn with toppings of your choice. Serve immediately.

CHAPTER 17

When You
Need a Helper

A Song of Ascents.
I will raise my eyes to the mountains; from where will my help come?
My help comes from the LORD, who made heaven and earth.
PSALM 121:1-2 NASB

For almost a decade, Brendan and I celebrated Christmas by escaping the smog of Los Angeles for the clean air of the Smoky Mountains. I grew up gazing at the shifting sand dunes of Dubai, so the permanence and majesty of these mountains sent my heart soaring. While the signature wisps of smoke on the peaks look like transparent locks of iridescent hair from below, from above, they look much different, more like thick mounds of marshmallow fluff atop a steaming cup of hot chocolate.

My in-laws' cabin sat on such a peak. Every morning a thick blanket of clouds rushed into the valley below us, obscuring every tree and turn beneath. A handful of mountain peaks, including ours, poked through the fluff, like bobbing heads in the ocean surf. I stood on the deck, sipping my coffee, in awe of this rarified air. Yet I was also struck by the poignant truth that, in a week I'd be back down there, living beneath the blinding cover, focused so much on the problems in front of me that I'd forget about the splendor above.

> We were never meant to do it alone.

The irony is that we're all this way. We're all drowning in the powerful currents of ambition and responsibility. Our culture cheers on the mavericks who scale the steep mountainside on their own, defying gravity or any other tethering to the earth below. And so we think we should be the same. We crawl through the valley on our own. A chorus chants in the background: you can have everything if you'd just plan more, work out more, sleep more, follow this guru, read this book . . . If we do acknowledge we need help, we look to ourselves or to others rather than to the One who made the heavens and the earth.

We were never meant to do it alone. In the Garden, God looked at Adam and said, "It is not good that man should be alone; I will make him a helper comparable to him" (Genesis 2:18 NKJV). Centuries later, Jesus would look at His helpless, scared disciples and promise, "The Helper will come—the Spirit, who reveals the truth about God and who comes from the Father. I will send Him to you from the Father, and He will speak about Me." (John 15:26 GNT).

God is not only able to give us a helper but He also wants to. He knows we're prone to keeping our eyes fixed on the environment around us. We look to the ground, afraid that we'll drop everything we're juggling if we look away. (And who's going to clean it up? Well, because we're on our own, we will. Add another task to the to-do list!) But what if help was already here, standing right by our side? What if all we had to do to be helped was look up?

In ancient Middle Eastern culture, the mountaintops were considered home to the deities, perhaps because from that high vantage point, the gods could see everything. From Moses to Jesus Himself, the Israelites scaled mountains to get as physically close to God as possible. It's there that God delivered the Ten Commandments and where Jesus communed with Moses and Elijah. Even the temple was built on Mount Moriah in Jerusalem, which was set amidst the hilly country of Judea.

When the psalmist lifts his eyes to the mountains, maybe he's longing for the closeness to the Lord that comes from being in the temple. And yet he reminds himself that God's help is not restricted to the four walls of the temple. No, our God,

> **What if all we had to do to be helped was look up?**

who made heaven and earth, is as close as "your shade on your right hand" (Psalm 121:5 NASB). Sometimes I have a hard time asking for God's help and blessing because I feel like I haven't earned it. I'm sleeping in instead of reading my Bible; I've indulged in behavior unbecoming to one who loves the Lord. Here is a reminder that perfection is not a precursor to His rescue. We don't need to be on the mountaintop in order to call out to Him. In fact, when it feels like our troubles are all-encompassing, swirling around us like a thick blanket of clouds, when we're exhausted by the responsibilities God has given us, all we have the power to do is, like the psalmist, lift our eyes! And guess what? That's all it takes! God comes rushing off the mountaintop, smoke billowing from His nostrils, His voice thundering from heaven.

> *He reached down from heaven and rescued me;*
> *He drew me out of deep waters.*
> **PSALM 18:16 NLT**

By the time I'd poured my second cup, the sun had usually started to rise over that Carolina vista. The warm rays shone down on the impenetrable miasma of marshmallow mist, prying it apart to reveal first an outline of a tree, then the branches. Within an hour, the mist had evaporated, and the sun illuminated what had once lain in darkness. It had melted the Smoky right off the mountains! What a reminder that a rising Son not only shines through the darkness but also eviscerates it. We need only lift up our eyes. Our Helper is already here.

> Our God, who made heaven and earth, is as close as "your shade on your right hand"
>
> (PSALM 121:5 NASB).

YOUR TURN

As you take a bite out of your smoky marshmallow brownies, read through Psalm 18. Is God angry as He comes to the psalmist's rescue because He doesn't want to be bothered or because He's fiercely protective over His child? How does it make you feel to know that the Creator, the most powerful one in all of existence, loves you so much that He's enraged when someone or something threatens your peace? See if you can sense Him chomping at the bit to help you!

Drinking Chocolate with Chili, Smoke, and Clouds

MAKES 4 SERVINGS | **TOTAL TIME:** 10 MINUTES | **ACTIVE TIME:** 10 MINUTES

Cook's Note: Jaggery is unrefined cane sugar, used widely in South Asian cooking. You can find it at Indian grocery stores, but a fine substitute would be dark brown sugar.

3 cups water

4 ounces unsweetened chocolate (70% cacao), chopped (recommended: Guittard)

3 tablespoons jaggery (see Cook's Note) or dark brown sugar

3 tablespoons creamy almond butter (unsalted)

1 teaspoon garam masala

¼ teaspoon kosher salt

¼ teaspoon chipotle chili powder

¼ teaspoon Aleppo pepper or cayenne pepper

Jarred marshmallow creme

1. Heat water in a small saucepan to 100 degrees Fahrenheit.

2. Pour hot water into your blender. Add the chocolate and cover. Allow to sit for 2 to 3 minutes, until chocolate is softened.

3. Now add jaggery, almond butter, garam masala, salt, chipotle chili powder, and Aleppo pepper.

4. Cover, hold lid in place, and blend on high until smooth.

5. Pour into 4 mugs. Using a small spoon, scoop up some marshmallow creme and drop spoon into a mug. Allow to sit for 30 seconds or so; the marshmallow creme will melt off the spoon and rise to the surface like a perfect little cloud. Repeat with remaining mugs. Sprinkle with salt and a little more Aleppo pepper if you like. Serve.

CHAPTER 18

When You Need Fuel for the Day

Not until you have your coffee teeth!" That is what Mum would say when I asked if I could also have a cup of coffee or tea in the mornings. Once all my "milk teeth" (baby teeth) had fallen out, in her mind, my body was mature enough to handle the highs and lows of caffeine.

Our souls need daily nourishment.

The allure still holds. While I've switched over to matcha (a type of green tea) as my morning beverage, I still look forward to that first sip with the same glee that I looked forward to my very first sip of coffee ever!

I wager the ritual of that first morning sip is shared and savored by so many because it's not about just the flavor—it's about a subconscious recognition that the time for slumber is over. A day of promise and opportunity awaits us—it's both exciting and intimidating. That morning cuppa is a cuppa courage, strengthening our spirit, focusing our vision, amping up our energy for all that God has written for us that day.

> *Besides this you know the time, that the hour has come for you to wake from sleep. For salvation is nearer to us now than when we first believed.*
>
> ROMANS 13:11 ESV

Our souls need daily nourishment.

Whether your day is daunting in a whole new way, or daunting in its never-ending same-ness, it's okay to feel like we need fuel to face it. God makes His mercies new every morning, because yesterday's nourishment often seems stale to us.

It's funny: with a rumbling of the tummy, our bodies tell us when we need more calories. A parched tongue tells us we're dehydrated. But my soul doesn't flash an indicator light when it's on empty. I don't realize that it needs nourishing on the same daily basis that my body does. Usually, by the time I realize that it's time for some serious quiet time with the Lord, I've already gotten hangry. I've spun out, done some things I probably regret, and find myself teary before the Lord. "Where are you?"

It's important to God that we aren't weary. We cannot be weary, because there's so much God has for us to do. This is vital work, the real stuff that underpins our careers, family, friendships, charity work. God is at work through us and in us.

And let us not grow weary of doing good, for in
due season we will reap, if we do not give up.
GALATIANS 6:9 ESV

> # God is at work through us and in us.

What's our fuel? My fitness friends swear that drinking a liter of water and then eating a carb-heavy breakfast helps them have a better morning workout. Jesus suggested we build our spiritual meals around God—focusing our minds on His reality, what He's doing, and what He's asking from us. We should delight ourselves in Him and fill our bellies to bursting!

Seek the Kingdom of God above all else, and live righteously,
and He will give you everything you need.
MATTHEW 6:33 NLT

Sure, we could grab a muffin or my favorite, a croissant. But a few hours later, I find myself hungry again. That food did not nourish, did not fuel. Similarly, when we fill ourselves on the Word and works of God, our souls are charged up, ready to go because this is actually the food that our souls need.

There are lots of other food sources vying for our attention, both destructive and good. We must eat the right things, in the right servings, and the right order!

Listen carefully to Me, and eat what is good, and your soul
will delight in the richest of foods. Incline your ear and
come to Me; listen, so that your soul may live.
ISAIAH 55:2-3 BSB

So what's in your spiritual morning cup? What's fueling you? Have you been skirting by on the bare minimum? Or is that cup full of the richest, deepest brew available on this side of eternity? (Oh my goodness, I just imagined what coffee tastes like in heaven. OH. MY. GOSH. Can you imagine?) Is your morning cuppa a blend of different beans, or is it single-origin? Is it from the source, cultivated and harvested by the grower Himself? Or is someone/something else getting in the way? Because anything less than that morning brew is not what your soul needs to thrive. Jesus came not only to shake us out of our slumber but also to raise us from

Jesus came not only to shake us out of our slumber but also to raise us from the dead.

the dead. He didn't just come to give us new life but life abundant! He doesn't just say to us, Wake up! No, my dear one, He draws the curtains, pulls off the covers, hands us a cup of His signature brew, and says, "(insert your name here), it's time to RISE AND SHINE!"

Sweet Potato Poutine with Red Eye Gravy

MAKES 4 TO 6 SERVINGS | **TOTAL TIME:** 50 MINUTES | **ACTIVE TIME:** 25 MINUTES

1 20-ounce bag frozen sweet potato nuggets

Avocado oil cooking spray

Gravy:

8 ounces Mexican-style pork chorizo

½ medium onion, finely chopped (about 100g)

4 tablespoons unsalted butter

¼ cup all purpose flour

½ cup brewed coffee

1 cup chicken stock

¼ cup heavy cream

Kosher salt and pepper

½ teaspoon red wine vinegar

½ cup queso fresco or feta cheese

2 to 3 scallions, white and green parts sliced finely on the diagonal

¼ cup finely chopped cilantro leaves and soft stems

2 to 3 radishes, sliced very thinly

1 lime, cut into wedges

1. Preheat oven to 425 degrees Fahrenheit, or temperature specified on sweet potato nuggets package. Line a sheet pan with parchment paper and spray with avocado oil. Lay sweet potato nuggets on the sheet pan, making sure they're spaced out evenly. When oven reaches correct temperature, bake the nuggets, adding an extra 10 to 15 minutes, until bottoms of the nuggets blacken slightly. Remove from the oven, sprinkle with a little salt and pepper, and set aside.

2. Meanwhile, make the gravy: Squeeze chorizo out of the package into a 10-inch cast iron skillet. Set over medium heat, and cook until chorizo softens and begins to release its fat.

3. Stir well, and add onions. Cook, making sure to spread the mixture evenly across base of skillet, pushing down a little to encourage the chorizo to start crisping up, 5 to 7 minutes. Flip the chorizo over to encourage the other side to crisp up too.

4. Sprinkle with flour and cook, stirring often, for 2 to 3 minutes.

5. Now add coffee and stock. Cook until mixture begins to thicken.

6. Finish with cream. Season with salt, pepper, and red wine vinegar. Set aside.

7. To serve, pull nuggets together into a pile on the sheet pan. Ladle gravy over the top. Sprinkle with cheese, scallions, cilantro, and radishes, and squeeze a couple of lime wedges over the top. Serve immediately!

CHAPTER 19

When You Need Strength

She is clothed with strength and dignity,
and she laughs without fear of the future.
PROVERBS 31:25 NLT

R ead that again.

Is that you?

No? Sometimes? Not today, though, huh? Me neither. Is it hard to read through tears? It's blurry right now for me too.

BTW, did you know that reading silently is a relatively new thing? St. Augustine was a theologian and philosopher who lived in the late sixth century. He is known as one of the most important church fathers of the Latin church in the Patristic Period. In his book, *Confessions*, St. Augustine wrote this about St. Ambrose, the man who converted and baptized him:

"But when Ambrose used to read, his eyes were drawn through the pages, while his heart searched for its meaning; however, his voice and tongue were quiet. Often when we were present—for anyone could approach him and it was not his habit that visitors be announced to him—we saw him reading in this fashion, silently and never otherwise."

> Our strength begins in our weakness!

Augustine remarked on this characteristic of Ambrose because it was, well, weird! Until about the seventeenth century, reading was a loud, social activity. The Scriptures, particularly the Old Testament, were passed primarily via oral tradition. And so these words weren't written to be read silently. These words were meant to ring in the atmosphere, to be heard not only by your ears but also by those around you.

I'm going to ask you to do something weird. You may feel uncomfortable but I urge you to push through. Read Proverbs 31:25 aloud. Replace "she" with "I" as in, "I am clothed in strength and dignity, and I laugh without fear of the future." Read it a few more times.

Where do you stumble? For me, it's the word "strength." I have moments of feeling strong, but honestly more often than not, I feel weak. The needs and challenges of my life seem so huge, and I am so small. Do you relate? If you and I were to sit and chat, I would probably use the word overwhelmed more than strong. And don't get me started on the future!

The Word of God can be confusing when it comes to strength!

But [God] said to me, "My grace is sufficient for you, for my power is made perfect in weakness." Therefore I will boast all the more gladly about my weaknesses, so that Christ's power may rest on me.

II CORINTHIANS 12:9 NIV

The Christian walk is one that embraces seeming contradictions: we surrender to find power, we gain freedom by being dependent, we have to be weak in order to be strong.

Our strength begins in our weakness!

So how does His strength manifest in our lives? God's strength is delivered via His grace to us. Sometimes grace removes that thing that makes us feel weak. Sometimes He leaves it there, as a thorn in our side. He strengthens us to shoulder that burden, so we appreciate on an intimate level, not a book-smart level, His strength . . . His miraculous power to make the difficult tolerable. We cannot experience or accept God's strength unless we experience our weakness, especially these days when there's a quick fix, a hack, available with the tap of a button on our phones. We cannot be under any illusion of our own self-sufficiency.

> Start with Him. Remember that we can't pull real strength from ourselves.

We can see in Proverbs 31 how we can clothe ourselves in strength and dignity. Look particularly at verse 30: The root of her strength is her fear of the Lord. We may be overwhelmed by the challenges before us, but those should not be the object of our fear or attention. Start with Him. Remember that we can't pull real strength from ourselves.

We take what little strength we have and we use it to love the Lord! We don't use it to fight our battles.

And you shall love the Lord your God with all your heart and with all your soul and with all your mind and with all your strength.

MARK 12:30 ESV

He in turn does what He does best: Like the fishes and loaves, He takes what little we have to offer and multiplies it beyond our wildest imagination and strength! Don't forget that we serve the God that promised:

> *When you pass through the waters, I will be with you; and through the rivers, they shall not overwhelm you; when you walk through fire you shall not be burned, and the flame shall not consume you.*
>
> ISAIAH 43:2 ESV

So now, try reading that verse from Proverbs aloud again. You don't need to feel strong. You are strong, because the God who parted the Red Sea and raised His Son from the dead has your back. He clothes you with His strength.

As you make tonight's meal, keep this verse in mind, "You shall love the Lord your God with all your heart and with all your soul and with all your mind and with all your strength" (Mark 12:30 ESV).

And think through these questions:

How can you love the Lord your God with all your strength right now?

Where do you feel His strength in your life today?

Where do you need His strength now? Ask Him for that strength.

When I first started to follow Christ, it felt like I was living in upside-down land! What I'd considered strength, I now saw had led to weakness. In God's topsy-turvy kingdom, true strength (His) is actually found in my own weakness. Control is found in dependency on Him. And so what better recipe to illustrate this concept than a muffin that buries the best part– tender, caramelized chunks of pineapple– at the bottom of the muffin!

> We take what little strength we have and we use it to love the Lord!

Pineapple Upside Down Corn Muffins

MAKES 12 MUFFINS | **TOTAL TIME:** 1 HOUR | **ACTIVE TIME:** 30 MINUTES

Pineapple:

Nonstick cooking spray, for the muffin pan

3 tablespoons dark brown sugar

2 tablespoons unsalted butter

¼ teaspoon ground allspice

¼ teaspoon kosher salt

⅛ teaspoon ground cinnamon

2 cups fresh pineapple, cut into ½-inch pieces

Muffins:

½ cup boiling water

½ cup fine yellow cornmeal

¾ cup buttermilk

1 large egg, lightly beaten

½ cup all-purpose flour

1 tablespoon granulated sugar

1 teaspoon baking powder

½ teaspoon kosher salt

¼ teaspoon baking soda

Flaky sea salt, for garnish

1. For the pineapple: Preheat the oven to 450 degrees Fahrenheit. Grease a 12-cup muffin pan with cooking spray. Combine the brown sugar, butter, allspice, kosher salt, and cinnamon in a skillet over medium-low heat and cook until bubbling. Add the pineapple, stir to coat, and cook until the liquid has nearly evaporated and the caramel has deepened in color, about 7 minutes.

2. For the muffins: Meanwhile, working quickly, whisk the boiling water into the cornmeal in a large bowl until you get a stiff mash. Whisk in the buttermilk, stirring until smooth. Stir in the egg, then add the flour, granulated sugar, baking powder, kosher salt, and baking soda and mix until just incorporated.

3. Add 2 to 3 pieces of the pineapple to the bottom of each muffin cup. Evenly divide the cornbread mixture among the muffin cups, filling each three-quarters of the way full.

4. Bake for 15 minutes. Cool on a wire rack for 5 minutes. Use a paring knife to remove each muffin, flipping it to reveal the caramelized pineapple before placing on a plate. Sprinkle with flaky sea salt and serve!

CHAPTER 20

When You Need the Presence of God

We are a notoriously touchy-feely family. Physical contact is one of most sturdy steadiers in our unsteady home. Our girls request cuddle sessions in our bed to help heal everything from hurt feelings to a skinned knee. If you and I met, at some point I would probably reach out and rub your arm. And my husband, who hugs everyone he meets (even strangers), started at a young age, when he tried to melt a grumpy grandparent's icy heart by reaching out his arms and saying, "But I'm a huggy buggy!"

And so perhaps it makes sense that when I sit down to pray, I'll often include the line: "I just need a touch, some sense of Your presence, Lord. Then I can do anything."

Faith, Martin Luther King Jr. said, is taking the first step even when you don't see the whole staircase. In our case, it's throwing our lives behind the all-knowing, all-powerful, present-everywhere-at-the-same-time Creator of all . . . even though He's invisible.

"No one has ever seen God; the only God, who is at the Father's side, He has made Him known" (John 1:18 ESV).

I'm comforted that even Moses, who had as close a face-to-face conversation with Yahweh as anyone in history, begged for the same thing:

"'If your presence does not go,' Moses responded to Him, 'don't make us go up from here. How will it be known that I and your people have found favor with you unless you go with us? I and your people will be distinguished by this from all the other people on the face of the earth'" (Exodus 33:15–16 CSB).

Did you catch that? Moses recognized that as children of God, our special privilege is that God walks with us.

God's presence brings rest (see v. 14) and reassures us of His favor and protection. It gives us our identity.

David was no stranger to God's presence. Saul, the first king of Israel, was said to be afraid of David, his soon-to-be successor, because "the LORD was with him" (I Samuel 18:12 ESV). He knew that presence was not only a place to run to, hide in, rest upon . . . but even more powerfully, it was inescapable!

> *Where shall I go from your Spirit? Or where shall I flee from your presence?*
> *If I ascend to heaven, you are there! If I make my bed in Sheol, you are there!*
> *If I take the wings of the morning and dwell in the uttermost parts of the sea,*
> *even there your hand shall lead me, and your right hand shall hold me.*
> PSALM 139:7-10 ESV

God's presence is not simply surveillance, it's leading, directing, comforting. But if His presence is everywhere, why can't I see it? Sense it?

If we are His, His presence is with us whether we sense it or not.

Look again at the psalm. David refers to His presence as His Spirit. The Hebrew is *ruach* and, happily, it's one of my favorite kinds of words: onomatopoeia. It sounds just like what it means! *Ruach* equals "wind, breath, exhalation." Say it with me: *ruach!* (The "ch" sound comes from the back of your throat, kind of like you're coughing.)

Aha! Clues! Where else do we hear about God's breath?

> *Then the LORD God formed a man from the dust of the ground and breathed*
> *into his nostrils the breath of life, and the man became a living creature.*
> GENESIS 2:7 ESV

Later, Jesus followed in His Father's footsteps and breathed, ruach'd, the Holy Spirit onto the disciples. When God breathed on dust, it became a living human. When Jesus breathed on image bearers like you and me, they were transformed into vessels of the Holy Spirit.

In the Book of Acts, Paul says, "(God) Himself gives to all mankind life and breath and everything" (Acts 17:25 ESV). Are you breathing? That's something of God's Spirit that you can feel right now. Blow on your hand. You can feel it. His presence is inherent to your presence!

As you slide these pooris into the hot oil, and watch as they puff up with hot air (and joy!), consider the similarities to the way God made you. He packed you with every ingredient necessary for your role: flour, water, seasoning. Just as you kneaded air into the poori dough, so did He infuse us with His holy breath from the very beginning, and it's not going

> God's presence is not simply surveillance, it's leading, directing, comforting.

anywhere. And when do we see that rising agent working its hardest? Once the poori encounters the excruciating heat of the hot oil! Sometimes it's easier to sense God's presence when we're under severe stress, when we're at the very end of ourselves!

Every time you breathe you experience a gift of God! Don't feel the presence of God? Breathe. You just felt it.

"Late have I loved you, beauty so old and so new: late have I loved you. And see, you were within and I was in the external world and sought you there, and in my unlovely state I plunged into those lovely created things which you made. You were with me, and I was not with you. The lovely things kept me far from you, though if they did not have their existence in you, they had no existence at all. You called and cried out loud and shattered my deafness. You were radiant and resplendent, you put to flight my blindness. You were fragrant, and I drew in my breath and now pant after you. I tasted you, and I feel but hunger and thirst for you. You touched me, and I am set on fire to attain the peace which is yours" (St. Augustine).

Changing the way we breathe is a wonderful way to still ourselves and experience the presence of God. Have you ever practiced square breathing? The Navy Seals are said to use it ahead of a stressful maneuver, so if it's good enough for them, it's good enough for me! Wanna try it with me? Here's how it goes:

Inhale through your nose for 4 steady counts: 1, 2, 3, 4

Hold it for 4 counts

Exhale for 4 counts

Hold for 4 counts

Repeat 4 more times

How do you feel? A little calmer? Were you able to sense His presence? Sometimes, when I do this, it's almost like I can feel Jesus' cheek right next to mine. He's like, *Here I am. I've been here all along. Miss me?* (I imagine Jesus has a bit of a cheeky sense of humor, don't you?). As you cook today's recipe, think through what God's presence feels like to you!

> # Every time you breathe you experience a gift of God!

Pooris and Chana Masala (Indian Fried Bread with Spiced Chickpea Curry)

MAKES 4 TO 6 SERVINGS | **TOTAL TIME:** 1 HOUR 30 MINUTES | **ACTIVE TIME:** 45 MINUTES

Cook's Note: Atta is a stone-ground whole wheat flour used to make all manner of flatbreads throughout the Subcontinent. You can substitute with equal parts all-purpose flour and whole wheat flour. Ajwain seeds are often added to deep fried foods to aid digestion; they taste like thyme! You can find them at Indian stores or online.

Pooris

1 cup atta (see Cook's Note)

1 teaspoon ghee or avocado oil

1 teaspoon kosher salt

¼ teaspoon ajwain (carom) seeds (see Cook's Note)

½ cup warm water, plus more as needed

Peanut or other oil for frying

Chana Masala

1 teaspoon coriander seeds

2 teaspoons cumin seeds, divided

2 tablespoons ghee, or avocado oil

2 to 3 dried bay leaves

2 black cardamom pods, gently crushed open

1 medium yellow onion (200g), finely chopped

6 cloves garlic, grated on a microplane or minced, about 1½ teaspoons

2-inch piece ginger, grated on a microplane or minced, about 1½ teaspoons

½ teaspoon garam masala

¼ Kashmir chili powder, or sweet paprika

¼ teaspoon turmeric

1 13.76-ounce carton crushed tomatoes (a little over 1 cup)

2 15-ounce cans chickpeas, drained but not rinsed

1¼ cup hot water

Kosher salt and pepper

2 teaspoons lemon juice

Handful of minced cilantro leaves and soft stems

1. Make poori dough: In a large bowl, work atta, ghee, kosher salt, and ajwain seeds together with your fingertips until well combined. Now, slowly drizzle in water, a little at a time, until a firm dough forms. Knead for a couple of minutes, then place in the bowl, cover with a damp towel, and allow to rest for at least 15 minutes.

2. Make chana masala: Buzz coriander seeds and 1 teaspoon cumin seeds in a spice grinder to make a fine powder. Warm ghee or oil in a large nonstick wok or deep skillet. Once shimmering, add bay leaves, black cardamom pods, and remaining 1 teaspoon whole cumin seeds. Cook until they're fragrant, about 30 seconds.

3. Now add onion, season with a pinch of salt, and cook until softened and translucent, 5 to 10 minutes. Drop in grated garlic and ginger, add a pinch of salt, and cook another 2 minutes, until the raw fragrance diminishes.

4. Now sprinkle in ground coriander mixture, garam masala, Kashmir chili powder, and turmeric. Cook, stirring frequently for about 20 seconds. Add a splash of water and cook another 30 seconds until glossy.

5. Add crushed tomatoes along with, you guessed it, a pinch of salt. Stir well, and cook until tomatoes soften, and the whole mixture thickens. You're looking for a specific sign here: the whole mixture (the masala) will hold together when you pull it towards the center, rather than spread back out, and little bubbles of ghee will sizzle around the perimeter of the mixture. The mixture will darken in color too.

6. Tumble in the chickpeas and toss to ensure every legume is covered in the masala. Cook for 1 minute.

7. Add 1 cup hot water. Turn the heat up to bring the pot to a boil. Now turn heat down to a simmer, cover, and cook for 30 minutes, until chickpeas soften and curry reduces a little.

8. Stir in lemon juice, and taste, adding salt as you feel necessary. Garnish with cilantro, cover and set side until you've made the pooris.

9. Warm frying oil in a large dutch oven over medium heat to 350 degrees Fahrenheit.

10. Divide dough into 8 portions, rolling each into a ball. Squish a portion into a level puck, then quickly dunk in extra flour. Roll into a 4- to 5-inch circle. Flap the circle from one hand to another to remove excess flour, then carefully drop into the hot oil. The poori round should sink to the bottom, then quickly rise to the surface. Using a spid0er or slotted spoon, gently but insistently nudge the poori to encourage it to puff up. Once puffed, carefully flip it over and cook the other side for 30 seconds or so. Remove to paper towel–lined plate and repeat with remaining dough. Pooris are best when eaten hot! Serve with chana masala.

Every time
you breathe,
you experience
a gift from God!
Don't feel the
presence of God?
Breathe.
You just felt it.

SECTION 03

When You Need to Wind Down

CHAPTER 21

When You Need Peace

*Be anxious for nothing, but in everything by prayer and supplication,
with thanksgiving, let your requests be made known to God.
And the peace of God, which surpasses all understanding, will
guard your hearts and your minds in Christ Jesus.*

PHILIPPIANS 4:6-7 NKJV

I grew up in Dubai; the traditional Arabic greeting wasn't hello. It was (and still is) *As-salamu Alaikum*, which means, "Peace be with you." The correct response is, *Wa Alaikum Assalam*, which means, "And peace be with you also."

Even saying goodbye (*Ma'a salama*) carried a deeper meaning: "Go in peace." It's similar in Jewish culture. Inherently, coming into or leaving someone's presence is a recognition of the one thing every human is always looking for: peace.

Jesus said the following: "Peace I leave with you; My peace I give you. I do not give to you as the world gives. Do not let your hearts be troubled and do not be afraid" (John 14:27 NIV). When He said this, He distinguished His peace by making clear that the kind He gives is not the world's version.

> He is the Prince of Peace.

Too often we grab at the counterfeit peace mantras that litter social media: "I may not be all that they need, but I'm enough," "Do what feels right," and "Follow your heart" (which is the one that always gets me in trouble when I adopt it). All of these rely on our own estimation of things, but that's what got us into trouble in the first place.

We were actually built for a far superior version of peace: the peace of God, which surpasses all understanding. It burrows deep and does a deeper work—guarding our hearts and minds from further panic. So if you want a piece of that peace, look nowhere else but the feet of Jesus. He is the Prince of Peace. Ask early and often. Ask with a grateful heart, knowing that what He achieved on the cross was shalom, real peace. It's not simply an absence of trouble, but wholeness, completeness, and everything-as-it-should-be. It was what we were made for. Anything less will never satisfy!

Lord, I am desperate for the kind of peace that only You can give. I don't want fluffy ideas and inspirational quotes—I want the real thing. Thank You for the work that You accomplished on the cross so that I could experience wholeness and satisfaction in You. When I am weak, You are strong. Your Word is a lamp to my feet and a light to my path. When my spirit faints within me, You know my way. Please take this burden of anxiety that I've been carrying around. Fill my heart with the richness of Your shalom. Amen.

If there's one dish that unites the Middle East, it's probably hummus. And yet, when I came to the States, I was dismayed at what was passing for hummus at the grocery store. The hummus of my youth was light, velvety, like a cloud of chickpea and sesame. So I set out to create a recipe that would approximate the real thing because when you've tasted the real thing, just like when you've experienced true shalom, nothing else will do.

> Lord, I am desperate for the kind of peace that only You can give.

Warm Hummus with Spiced Ground Lamb and Endive Salad

MAKES 4 SERVINGS | **TOTAL TIME:** 45 MINUTES | **ACTIVE TIME:** 45 MINUTES

Cook's Note: Za'atar is a bright, herby, sour spice blend you'll find in kitchens across the Middle East. You can find it at gourmet markets, Middle Eastern and Asian grocery stores, and online. You can substitute with equal parts dried thyme, dried oregano, sesame seeds, and lemon zest. Feel free to use good store-bought hummus if you don't want to make it yourself.

Spiced lamb

1 pound ground lamb

1 teaspoon ground allspice

1 teaspoon za'atar (see Cook's Note)

½ teaspoon ground cinnamon

2 tablespoons chopped mint leaves

2 tablespoons chopped parsley

3 tablespoons olive oil

Quick Hummus

2 15-ounce cans chickpeas, drained, chickpea water retained

Kettle of boiling water

1 clove garlic, chopped

½ cup tahini

¼ cup lemon juice (about 1 lemon's worth)

6 ice cubes, standard 1 ounce cubes

Kosher salt and freshly ground pepper

Whole wheat pita bread for serving

Extra lemon wedges for serving

Salad

¼ cup parsley leaves

¼ cup mint leaves, torn

¼ cup lemon juice (about 1 lemon's worth)

2 endives, washed and sliced

2 to 4 dried apricots, soaked in hot water for 10 minutes, minced about 2 tablespoons

¼ cup toasted pine nuts or chopped almonds

1. Marinate lamb: Mix lamb, allspice, za'atar, cinnamon, mint, parsley, and 1 teaspoon kosher salt together until well combined. Cover and set aside on the counter for 30 minutes while you make the rest of the dish.

2. Measure out ¼ cup of chickpea water (also known as aquafaba) before draining the chickpeas and set aside. Tumble drained chickpeas into a large bowl and cover with hot water by a couple of inches. Allow to rest for 15 minutes.

3. Now make the hummus: Drain warm chickpeas and immediately pour them into your food processor. Buzz for 2 to 3 minutes until smooth paste forms.

4. Add the reserved aquafaba, garlic, tahini, lemon juice, ice cubes, and 1 teaspoon salt. Buzz for 5 minutes until a smooth, fluffy hummus comes together. Taste for seasoning, adjusting salt, lemon juice, and tahini as you like. Spoon hummus onto your serving platter. Use the back of your spoon to create a large pool where the lamb will sit. Set aside.

5. Make the salad: Toss everything together in a medium bowl, seasoning with salt and pepper. Set aside.

6. Cook lamb: Heat olive oil in a large cast iron skillet over medium-high heat until shimmering. Add the lamb and cook until browned on the bottom, 4 to 5 minutes, then flip and cook other side until browned, 4 to 5 minutes more. Stir and use the edge of your spatula to break it all up. Taste for seasoning, then spoon the warm lamb into the hollow you created in the hummus. Spoon the endive and apricot salad over the lamb and hummus. Serve with lots of warm pita bread and lemon wedges.

CHAPTER 22

When You Need Calm in the Chaos

"Be still, and know that I am God."
PSALM 46:10 NIV

At no other time in history have humans had access to as much input as we do right now. We can peer into literally hundreds of people's lives every day, looking through the window panes of our phones. Not only that, but neighbors, coworkers, and family members can contact us any time, day or night. Personally, it doesn't take much for my carefully controlled reality to crack under the strain. One series of woeful headlines, one child's tantrum, or one burned pan and . . . I'm drowning. Can you relate?

I know I'm not the only one to experience this. When the disciples of Jesus got caught in a wild storm on the sea of Galilee, they panicked. But more than that, they were mad that their Master didn't even seem to care! He was asleep! On a cushion!

But Jesus was in the stern, sleeping on the cushion. So they woke Him and said, "Teacher, don't You care that we are perishing?" Then Jesus got up and rebuked the wind and the sea. "Silence!" He commanded. "Be still!" And the wind died down, and it was perfectly calm. "Why are you so afraid?" He asked. "Do you still have no faith?" Overwhelmed with fear, they asked one another, "Who is this, that even the wind and the sea obey Him?"
MARK 4:38-40 BSB

> In order for us to find the calm in the storm, we must be still and sit with the Lord.

Jesus was in control the whole time. And even though we know Jesus is in control of our lives, we panic when we experience chaos. In order for us to find the calm in the storm, we must be still and sit with the Lord. Much as He lay on a cushion, lay your head on His chest. When you rest in Jesus, you acknowledge that He's on guard.

Nothing can creep up on you when He's on duty! He is sovereign, not just over us, but over every ounce of creation.

PRAY WITH ME

Lord, help me to recognize Your power. Help me to stop playing God, to stop worrying about the past, present, and future, to stop running to counterfeit shelters, and to stop looking for others to solve my problems for me. Give me the willingness to be still with You and rest in Your love and faithfulness. You are my fortress. You are my refuge and strength, my very present help in trouble. I have no more reasons to be afraid, because You are with me, and You will help me. Thank You for being the same yesterday, today, and forever.

In one of my favorite shows, *Yellowstone*, the main character often feels like he's warring against the world. The future of his ranch and his family weighs heavily on his shoulders, and he's constantly trying to control the chaos. And so I found it so endearing when, searching for a bit of comfort, he goes to the local diner for some Salisbury steak and mashed potatoes; it's a plate of humble comfort that requires him to let go of the reins for a few moments. I hope it does the same for you.

> When you rest in Jesus, you acknowledge that He's on guard.

Salisbury Steak and Massaman Gravy

MAKES 4 SERVINGS | **TOTAL TIME:** ABOUT 1 HOUR | **ACTIVE TIME:** 30 MINUTES

Cook's Note: Massaman curry is a mild Thai curry with roots in ancient Persia. My favorite brand of pre-prepared curry pastes is Maesri, which I find at Asian supermarkets and online. You could substitute Thai red curry paste if you like, but it will be much spicier!

1 14-ounce can full-fat coconut milk

7 tablespoons potato flakes (also known as instant mashed potatoes)

1 pound ground beef (90-10)

¾ teaspoon ground cumin

½ teaspoon garam masala

Kosher salt and freshly ground black pepper

¼ cup avocado oil (or other neutral oil)

2 tablespoons Massaman curry paste (recommended: Maesri brand)

1 pound white mushrooms, sliced thinly

1 tablespoon all-purpose flour

1 cup low-sodium beef stock

1 teaspoon tamarind paste (or 2 teaspoons lime juice)

1 tablespoon fish sauce

1 tablespoon white granulated sugar

1 cinnamon stick (optional)

1 star anise pod (optional)

1 Fresno chili (or other fresh red chili), finely sliced

¼ cup roasted salted peanuts, crushed or chopped

¼ cup chopped cilantro leaves and soft stems

Mashed potatoes or rice for serving

1. Whisk ½ cup of the coconut milk (not the whole can!) with potato flakes in a large bowl. Now add beef, ground cumin, garam masala, ½ teaspoon kosher salt, and as much freshly ground black pepper as you like. Knead until combined. Shape into four ½-inch-thick oval patties, and set on parchment-lined platter. Refrigerate for 30 minutes to firm up.

2. Warm 1 tablespoon oil in a large nonstick skillet over medium-high heat. Add meat patties and cook until well browned on each side, about 8 to 10 minutes total. Transfer to a clean plate to rest.

3. Now, lower the heat to medium and add remaining oil to skillet. Spoon in the curry paste and cook, stirring often,

until slightly deepened in color and very fragrant, about 3 minutes.

4. Add the mushrooms, season with salt, then cook until liquid has evaporated, about 5 minutes. Add the flour and cook another 2 minutes.

5. Stir in the remaining coconut milk, beef stock, tamarind paste, fish sauce, sugar, cinnamon stick, and star anise (if using). Bring back up to a simmer.

6. Lay the patties back in the gravy, and simmer on medium-low heat until cooked through, 12 to 15 minutes. Serve over mashed potatoes or rice and sprinkle the top with the fresno, peanuts, and cilantro.

CHAPTER 23

When You Need Rest

*"Come to Me, all you who are weary and burdened,
and I will give you rest."*
MATTHEW 11:28 NIV

One of the worst things you can be in Indian culture is lazy. I can't watch TV without doing something with my hands, whether it's crocheting or folding laundry. Every ounce of rest must be counteracted by some form of useful, practical work. Rest for the sake of rest is alien to me, even though I long for it.

American culture is not so different. The United States was founded on the notion that we can be whatever we want in life as long as we work hard . . . so you'd better get moving. Not getting ahead means you're falling behind. And yet our Lord values rest so much that He made us need sleep every night, and He commanded us to take one day a week off. So how do we rest in the way Jesus would have us rest?

Let's examine ourselves first. What burdens are we unduly putting on ourselves? What burdens have others unduly put on our shoulders too? What can we lay down at the Master's feet? Jesus called those who are weary. This isn't about being weary from a good day's work, it's about being weary from trying to justify ourselves, from finding our worth through work and endless striving. We can rest in Jesus because He's already done the real work. You no longer have to prove your value; you already have it in Him. That's what true rest looks like.

> You no longer have to prove your value; you already have it in Him.

While we all ought to take a weekly breather from our activities and careers—and go to sleep when we're tired, instead of turning to our screens—resting in Jesus means knowing that you matter just because you belong to Him. No amount of achievement can add to your value; no amount of criticism can detract from it. And that is worth an exhale!

PRAY WITH ME

Lord, thank You that I have all the rest I need in You. Thank You for setting me free from the toil and striving that will never yield the result I really want. Help me to engage in meaningful rest here on earth and anticipate the rest that I will enjoy in Your presence forever. Help me to recognize and fully absorb the rest that is waiting for me today when I choose to embrace all of who You are and what You've done. Thank You for doing the real work. Amen.

This recipe came about on a Sunday afternoon after church. I wanted a dish that wouldn't take all day, but also would feel snuggly, like a heavy blanket on a cold day. I knew we all needed a nap, and this was the dish to help us get there! As you drop the dumplings into the broth, imagining dropping your burdens down just for tonight. Just as the broth transforms that raw batter into something wonderful, imagine what the Lord can do when we find our rest in Him!

Saffron Chicken Korma and Dumplings

MAKES 4 TO 6 SERVINGS | TOTAL TIME: 1 HOUR | ACTIVE TIME: 1 HOUR

¼ cup full-fat coconut milk, warmed to body temperature

2 large pinches good quality saffron, about 2 teaspoons

¼ cup avocado oil (or other neutral oil)

1 large yellow onion, thinly sliced into half moons

¼ cup ghee or butter

4 carrots, slice ¼-inch thick

1 large bulb fennel, thick outer skin removed, cored, diced

2 teaspoons grated garlic

1 tablespoon grated ginger

3 bay leaves

1 tablespoon ground coriander

¼ teaspoon garam masala

¼ teaspoon Kashmir chili powder (or paprika; see note)

4 tablespoons all-purpose flour

¼ cup dry vermouth

4 cup low-sodium chicken broth

Meat from 1 rotisserie chicken, torn into bite-size pieces, about 6 cups

Kosher salt

Freshly ground black pepper

Dumplings

2 cups all-purpose flour

1 tablespoon baking powder

1 teaspoon kosher salt

1 cup full-fat coconut milk

1 cup frozen green peas, defrosted and warmed in microwave

¼ cup toasted flaked almonds

1. Pour warm coconut milk into a small bowl. Add saffron threads. Cover and allow to infuse.

2. Warm avocado oil in large Dutch oven set over medium-high heat, until shimmering. Add the onions, season with a pinch of salt, and fry gently, stirring occasionally, until golden brown, about 10 minutes. Using a slotted spoon, remove to paper towel–lined plate, leaving behind as much oil as possible. Pour oil off into a small bowl and set aside.

3. Melt the ghee in the Dutch oven. Add the carrots and fennel, season with a pinch of salt, and cook until softened, about 7 minutes. Add the grated garlic and ginger, along with the bay leaves, ground coriander, garam masala, and Kashmir chili powder; cook for

30 seconds, until no longer raw. Stir in 4 tablespoons flour, then whisk in vermouth, scraping up any browned bits.

4. Stir in broth, ¼ cup saffron-infused coconut milk and rotisserie chicken. Bring to a simmer, and cook, covered, over medium to medium-low heat about 10 minutes.

5. Make dumplings: Stir the flour, baking powder, and salt together in a medium bowl. Microwave the coconut milk and 3 tablespoons of reserved caramelized onion oil (adding more avocado oil if you don't have enough) in a microwave-safe bowl on high until just warm (do not over-heat), about 1 minute. Stir the warmed milk mixture into the flour mixture with a wooden spoon until incorporated and smooth.

6. Uncover stew, and season with salt and pepper. Pull out and remove bay leaves. Drop golfball-sized dumplings over the top of the stew, about ¼ inch apart (you should have about 18 dumplings). Reduce the heat to low, cover, and cook until the dumplings have doubled in size, 15 to 18 minutes. Sprinkle with caramelized onions, peas, and almonds. Serve.

CHAPTER 24

When You Need Patience

Patience is bitter, but its fruit is sweet.
ARISTOTLE

I am extraordinarily patient, provided I get my own way in the end.
MARGARET THATCHER

If you've been around church ladies for any length of time, you have undoubtedly heard some variation of this gem: "Don't pray for patience, darlin', because the Lord will teach it to you."

The first time I heard this, I realized that I had imagined that, upon requesting patience from the Lord, it would drop down from heaven like a serene white dove upon my head. Boop! Patience, delivered.

I much more relate to Margaret Thatcher than I do Aristotle! Hearing that aphorism was a rude awakening. So I can understand if you don't feel comfortable even holding this book in your hands right now! If I go looking for patience, will I only find it through fiery trials over an extended period of time? Or, if you've been praying for patience to deal with a particular person, won't constant exposure to that very person be God's likely course of action?

> Our King is undisturbed. His patience is infinite.

Well, you're not necessarily wrong. It might get worse before it gets better. But in the meantime, how much worse can it get in the five minutes it takes you to read this devotion? Patience! This might help!

Waiting is probably one of the hardest virtues to achieve, which means it's probably one of the most vital. (Don't you just hate how that works?)

When I lose my patience, I am most aware of my humanness, how starkly opposite I am to God, whose patience is long-suffering. He has been waiting on us since the beginning of time, maybe even before it, since He invented time and all. Our King is undisturbed. He's implacable. His patience is infinite.

Now, let's be honest: I'm assuming that whole knowing-the-future-because-He-wrote-it thing helps with patience. We don't have that luxury! And yet, doesn't our impatience also imply some level of God-delusion? Meaning, when we're impatient for God to act, doesn't that mean that somewhere in our minds, *we've* set the schedule? We've decided what's a reasonable time to wait for the resolution of a matter? That's humbling, right? Who are we to know how long a difficulty should last? Where were we when He hung the stars and all that?

Still, as a good parent, while He understands waiting is hard for us, He knows it's good for us, and so He tells us that we're going to have to do it.

> Wait for the LORD, and keep to His way, and He will exalt you to
> inherit the land; you will look on the destruction of the wicked.
> PSALM 37:34 NRSV

We might see patience as a submissive, passive act, but David makes it clear here that it's active! To be patient is to make a choice to trust His schedule over our own. This is a daily, maybe a minute-by-minute, choice because oh, how our own hearts want to wrestle the schedule back! The constant giving over, the daily repetition of "Thy will be done, not mine"—these are not small moves. These are defiant fists in the air of a world where personal autonomy rules.

> Who are we to know how long a difficulty should last? Where were we when He hung the stars?

The daily surrender not only strengthens our resolve to wait on Him, but it also leads to staying in His way, His Light, His Love. This too is active. We keep moving within the path that God has laid out for us to tread. We might be impatient right now because we're not just in the dark about the future—we're in the dark altogether! "Where are You, Lord?" we cry. And He says, "I'm here. In the Light. Where are you?" Keep to His way and you are where He is.

Waiting is inherently a tension. The Hebrew connects this word wait with the twisting and stretching of a strand of rope. Twisting and stretching make us stronger, more flexible, more mobile. In my workouts, I've learned that stretching and mobility are even more important than strength. It keeps me from getting hurt in the future as my bones grow more brittle. Tension is where growth happens. Something has to give.

What happens when we wait on Him and keep moving as He would have us move? "He will exalt you." He will lift us up! Hallelujah! Our patience yields sweet fruit indeed, not just in terms of building character (which, let's face it, isn't the best motivation when I'm in the thick of impatience), but also in terms of provision and safety. How often is our patience absent because of some threat to our provision and safety? He will take us there. God's Word is sure. If He says He will, He will.

Lastly, in the verse above (Psalm 37:34) . . . it gets a little dark, doesn't it? God doesn't mess around. David and his son Solomon were consumed with the seeming injustice of their enemies prospering, even when they ignored or mocked God, while the righteous suffered. Do you relate? It's hard to be patient in those circumstances, right? When all you can think is "Those guys! They got their cookies already!"

God promises that we will get to see justice but in His time. Not yours. Plus, He will do it in perfect righteousness, which neither you nor I can say we'll do.

Running out of patience, losing our patience . . . it can feel good in its moment to unleash, right? But then the afterglow fades and shame rushes in. We begin to compose our apology and we feel even more frustrated, only now in a defeated way, with shame flames dancing around the field of our vision as the anger dims.

> Daily surrender not only strengthens our resolve, but it also leads to staying in His way, His Light, His Love.

But for those who hold to the Way of the Lord, who wait with patience?

> *"Then you will know that I am the LORD; those who*
> *wait for me shall not be put to shame."*
> ISAIAH 49:23 NRSV

Now, since we don't pray for patience because we don't want to keep learning the hard way, let's start cooking a dish that will require—you betcha—a wee bit of patience. Come on, you knew it was heading that way, right?

Mussels Moilee
(with Coconut Milk and Turmeric)

MAKES 4 SERVINGS | **TOTAL TIME:** 30 MINUTES | **ACTIVE TIME:** 30 MINUTES

Cook's Note: Fresh curry leaves are an indispensable ingredient in South Indian cooking. I adore their signature scent of lemon verbena, anise, and a distinct savoriness that is hard to describe. I have yet to find a substitute, although makrut lime leaves come close. They are available at Indian grocery stores, and these days, I actually grow my own so I'm never without!

Cilantro-garlic toasts

8 tablespoons unsalted butter, softened

2 teaspoons grated garlic

2 tablespoons minced cilantro leaves and soft stems

Kosher salt and pepper

1 20-inch baguette, cut on bias into 1-inch slices

Mussels

2 pounds mussels, scrubbed and de-bearded

1 15-ounce can full-fat coconut milk

¼ cup water

1 teaspoon tamarind paste (or 2 teaspoon lime juice)

½ teaspoon dark brown sugar

2 tablespoons coconut or avocado oil

1 teaspoon black or brown mustard seeds

15 fresh curry leaves (2 to 3 sprigs; see Cook's Note)

2 medium shallots, thinly sliced

1 1-inch thumb ginger, sliced into matchsticks

1 teaspoon grated garlic

½ to 1 large jalapeño, minced (seeds and membranes removed if you don't like heat)

Good handful of cilantro, stems finely chopped, leaves chopped and kept separate, about 1 cup leaves and stems total

½ teaspoon turmeric

1 lime, sliced into wedges for serving

1. Adjust oven rack 5 inches from broiler element. Heat broiler. Combine butter, garlic, and cilantro in a small bowl, seasoning well with salt and pepper. Spread butter mixture on one side of baguette slices, then place, buttered side up, on a parchment-lined baking sheet.

2. Discard any mussels that do not close when gently tapped on the counter, or have a broken shell. Rinse in cold water, then set aside.

3. Whisk coconut milk, water, tamarind paste, and brown sugar together in a large measuring cup. Set aside.

4. Heat coconut oil in a large skillet over a medium flame until shimmering. Add the mustard seeds and curry leaves (watch out! The latter will splutter!). Stir and cook until mustard seeds start to pop, which should take just a few seconds.

5. Now add the sliced shallots and cook, stirring constantly, until softened but not browned, 2 to 3 minutes.

6. Stir in ginger, garlic, jalapeño, minced cilantro stems, and turmeric. Stir constantly for 30 seconds, until the raw aroma of the garlic and ginger dissipates.

7. Pour in the coconut milk mixture. Stir well and bring to a simmer. Add the cleaned mussels, cover and cook, stirring occasionally, until mussels open, 5 to 7 minutes. Discard any mussels that haven't opened.

8. Taste coconut milk-mussel broth for seasoning, and then turn off the heat, and sprinkle with fresh cilantro leaves. Broil baguette slices until lightly browned, about 1 minute. If you'd like, you can smear more butter on the reverse side, and broil for another minute. Serve with lime wedges for a final fresh spritz!

CHAPTER 25

When You Need to Slow Down

The LORD is my shepherd; I have what I need. He lets me lie down in green pastures; He leads me beside quiet waters. He renews my life; He leads me along the right paths for His name's sake.
PSALM 23:1-3 CSB

These days, my slowing down always has a purpose: ten minutes of meditation, watering the garden before it gets too hot, the surreptitious driveway social media scrolling that happens whenever I get home from errands (come on, I know you do it, too). Even in winding down, I feel the need to be productive or active. An inner restlessness keeps me moving, even though I desire the relief of just "being."

Psalm 23 sets a tranquil countryside scene. I take a deep breath every time I read it. I long for the peace of lush pasture, quiet waters, and some time in the sunshine with the Lord. But I confess that I also simultaneously think, *How long would I have to stay there? Like, forever?* I don't think I could last more than a few minutes before whining to the Lord, "Are we done here yet?"

So let's hear what David says when he imagines himself as a lamb in Jesus' care (Psalm 23:1-3). First, he isn't in charge anymore (as if he ever really was). He has no wants. He lies down in a place of growth and provision. He moves, following God, to places that quench his thirst but pose no danger. His soul and his energies are renewed. Resting and moving happen all at God's speed. God sets the pace. What I learn from this is that when I adjust my own gallop to His stroll through the garden, He unleashes the very relief and joy I've been scrambling to find—the One who keeps the world spinning, who raises the sun at its proper time, who drags it across the sky to its resting place every evening, at an intentional, patient, reliable pace. Let's set our clocks by Him.

> He unleashes the very relief and joy I've been scrambling to find.

PRAY WITH ME

Lord, help me to readjust my watch to Your timing. Let me follow You faithfully, like a sheep follows a shepherd, instead of running ahead and exhausting myself. Let me experience the joy and relief that come from simply being with You and letting You be in control. Give me faith that You are leading at just the speed I need to grow and follow You. Thank You for the gift of Your presence. Help me to slow down, see You clearly, and experience You fully. Amen.

Let's set our clocks by Him.

My friend Erin shared one of her favorite memories from childhood: When the temperatures would soar at the peak of the North Carolina summer, her grandmother would usher them all out to the rocking chairs on the porch, accompanied by glasses of ice cold sweet tea. It was a blessed time out, an acknowledgment that we all need to slow down, or plain ol' stop sometimes. I like to think she'd like this recipe, borne out of the story of those hot summers on the porch.

Sweet Tea Teriyaki Pork

MAKES 4 SERVINGS | **TOTAL TIME:** 1 HOUR 20 MINUTES | **ACTIVE TIME:** 1 HOUR

Pork marinade

2 1-pound pork tenderloins

4 teaspoons grated ginger
(from 2-inch thumb)

2 teaspoons grated garlic
(from 2 cloves)

¼ cup sake

2 teaspoon kosher salt

2 tablespoons avocado oil

Teriyaki sauce

4 black tea bags

1 cup sugar

½ cup sake

2 teaspoons soy sauce

Toasted sesame seeds

Scallions, sliced

1. Preheat oven to 450 degrees Fahrenheit. Line sheet pan with foil, place wire rack in sheet pan.

2. Whisk ginger, garlic, sake, salt, and avocado oil together in a small bowl. Pour into a zip-top bag, and add the pork tenderloins. Seal and rub marinade all over the pork. Set on the counter and marinate for 20 to 30 minutes while making the teriyaki sauce.

3. Drop tea bags into a small saucepan, along with 2 cups of water. Bring to a boil. Turn heat off, and steep tea for 5 minutes. Remove tea bags.

4. Add sugar, and bring back to a boil. Simmer for 5 minutes until slightly thickened.

5. Stir in sake and soy sauce. Bring to a boil, turn down to medium-high, and cook for 4 to 6 minutes, until reduced by half. Set aside.

6. Heat large cast iron skillet over medium high heat until just smoking. Wipe off excess marinade and add to the skillet. Cook until browned on all sides, 5 to 7 minutes. Set browned tenderloins on the wire rack, brush with teriyaki sauce, and bake until meat registers 140 degrees Fahrenheit in the center, 15 minutes.

7. Transfer meat to a platter, tent loosely with foil, and let rest for 5 minutes.

8. Slice, drizzle with sauce, and sprinkle with sesame seeds and scallions.

CHAPTER 26

When You Need Simplicity

We were at a picturesque tavern in Lugano, on the border of Italy and Switzerland. It was nearing autumn so wild porcini mushrooms were in season. Our server (also the chef's wife) mentioned that they had a special dish on the menu: in-season wild porcini mushrooms with pork. My dad was immediately interested.

"What else is in the dish?" he asked. (My dad may not cook but he knows more about cooking than he lets on.)

"Pork chops and porcini mushrooms," she said. My dad cocked his head. "That's it?"

"We can add some black pepper," she offered.

"Ah. Okay. Thanks," Dad answered, not wanting to push the matter but realizing that the Indian bandwidth for complexity in spicing is a bit wider than the Italian one.

See, even a basic dish like dal (soupy spiced lentils) in the Indian compendium calls for at least four spices. Okay, six including the garlic and ginger. Okay, honestly? Maybe more like eight when all's said and done.

> "Love the Lord your God with all your heart and with all your soul and with all your mind."
>
> MATTHEW 22:37 NIV

Simplicity, I've realized, is wildly subjective. I realized this more fully when I started to learn about French- and Italian-style cooking, which focuses on making the most of a few ingredients. It's an entirely different school of thought. Neither is better than the other. But simplicity means different things to, say, Julia Child, than it does to me.

That said, no matter what your default setting is as far as simplicity goes, there's no question that our plates are overly full. Making a decision as simple as where you might go for dinner involves checking at least three websites and maybe a couple of Instagram accounts. As a former journalist, I triple-check most every news story I read in an effort to get the most objective telling. Need a new blender? Not only will your phone probably start advertising different brands to you once you mention it, but there's also a plethora of review websites that offer their top five options based on whether you're going to use it primarily for smoothies, soups, or making your own peanut butter.

To put it in terms that make sense to my mind: We're throwing every ding-dang spice in the dal. It tastes muddy. Our palate numbs out. We crave simplicity.

So much so that we now have ASMR videos, or videos of cookie decorating. Sometimes I'll write out Scripture in cursive, and my inbox is flooded by people commenting on the "soothing" and "satisfying" nature of something as simple as loops and lines flowing out of a pen nib.

Our lives are a dizzying flurry of interests, priorities, opinions, and responsibilities. It feels like a thoroughly modern problem. But it isn't. Take for example the song "Simple Gifts"[2] written by Joseph Brackett in the 1800s. My husband introduced me to the song.

> 'Tis the gift to be simple, 'tis the gift to be free,
> 'Tis the gift to come down where I ought to be;
> And when we find ourselves in the place just right,
> 'Twill be in the valley of love and delight.
> When true simplicity is gained,
> To bow and to bend we shan't be ashamed,
> To turn, turn will be our delight,
> Till by turning, turning we come 'round right.

What does Christ say is the simplest thing? The Pharisees asked Him this question, hoping to catch Him in an impossible predicament. Of the 613 commandments God gave, how could you possibly categorize one above all? They came from God after all.

"Jesus replied, 'Love the Lord your God with all your heart and with all your soul and with all your mind'" (Matthew 22:37 NIV).

Jesus quotes the Shema, a couplet from Deuteronomy that had become a daily prayer in ancient Israel. Every Jew was obligated to speak the Shema every morning and every night. Jesus probably grew up saying it! I'm actually super thankful to the Pharisees for conspiring to catch Him out, because today, centuries later, Jesus' answer is refreshingly simple. He boiled down every commandment, every Bible story, even the gospel, to just one verse. Genius.

So, let's look at the Shema (pronounced sha-MAA).

. . . .

2 https://hymnary.org/hymn/RS2016/page/117

Who is it aimed at? You and me.

Who is the object of our focus? The Lord (our God, magistrate, sovereign, savior).

What must you do with your focus? Love Him.

How? With all your heart (your will), soul (your living energy), strength (intensity), and Jesus adds mind (ability to think).

That's it. That's your number one most important duty in the whole wide world.

Sound overly simplistic? Well, don't forget that His ways are higher than our ways. There have been many times when, overwhelmed by the competing priorities and responsibilities, not to mention challenges, in my life, I've come to God a muddy pile.

"Where do I even begin?" I sigh.

And every single time, He says the same thing: "First things first. Put Me at the top of the pyramid of everything begging for your attention, and watch how it all comes along in order behind Me."

He gave me a funny little visual of a mother duck and her babies; they may float for a while, each swimming this way and that following their own fancies, but when she quacks and starts to move, isn't it amazing how they all wiggle into a straight line behind her and follow her lead?

> ## Set your eyes on Him, dear heart, because everything else is below Him on the priority scale.

Let's go back to basics, and put first things first. God first, everything else second. This is a strategy that has definitely worked for me, and I have felt the complexities of life drag me down when I don't do it. Similarly, in the kitchen, sometimes I just need something as simple as a whole roasted head of cauliflower. Nothing complicated, and yet there's something kinda beautiful about it too, right?

Set your eyes on Him, dear heart, because everything else is below Him on the priority scale. It's such an all-encompassing demand that it, in and of itself, provides immeasurable clarity. Okay, somewhat measurable. All your heart. All your soul. All your mind. Just that. Y'know . . . simple.

Whole Roasted Cauliflower with Makhani Sauce (Gobi Musallam)

MAKES 4 SERVINGS | **TOTAL TIME:** 2 HOURS 30 MINUTES | **ACTIVE TIME:** 2 HOURS 30 MINUTES

2 small to medium heads of cauliflower, 4 to 5-inch diameter

½ cup avocado or vegetable oil

1 teaspoon ground turmeric

1 teaspoon paprika

Kosher salt + freshly ground pepper

Makhani sauce

2 tablespoons ghee

4 to 5 cloves garlic, grated

1 pinkie's worth (20g) ginger, grated

2 bay leaves

26.46-ounce carton passata or strained tomatoes

2 cups water

¾ teaspoon paprika

¼ teaspoon Kashmir chili powder

1 teaspoon garam masala

1 tablespoon honey

1 tablespoon granulated white or cane sugar

1 teaspoon ground cumin

1 teaspoon dried fenugreek leaves

Fresh dill and cilantro, roughly chopped

¼ cup heavy cream

2 tablespoons butter

1. Preheat oven to 375 degrees Fahrenheit. Set oven rack in the middle of the oven. Set a wire rack in a parchment or aluminum foil–lined baking sheet. Set aside.

2. Stir together the oil, turmeric, and paprika. Using hands, rub the mixture all over the heads of cauliflower, making sure to get underneath. Sprinkle generously all over with salt and pepper. Pop the cauliflowers on the rack-lined baking sheet. Cover very well with foil, sealing edges, and bake for 40 minutes.

3. Remove the foil. Place a small baking dish of boiling water on the rack below the cauliflower. Roast for another 45 minutes to an hour, until the cauliflower is golden brown and tender. Remove from oven. Turn oven off.

4. Warm ghee in a large nonstick skillet or wok, set over medium-high heat. Add the garlic, ginger, and bay leaves; cook until fragrant, about 30 seconds.

5. Now add passata, water, paprika, Kashmir chili powder and 1 teaspoon kosher salt. Stir together, bring to a

boil, then turn down to a simmer. Cover and cook for 20 minutes.

6. Stir in garam masala, honey, sugar, cumin, dried fenugreek leaves, and a small handful of dill and cilantro, about 2 tablespoons each. Cover and cook another 15 minutes.

7. Stir in cream and butter. Simmer another 5 minutes. Taste for seasoning.

8. To serve: Turn broiler on. Place cauliflower heads in an oven-safe skillet or dish. Pour sauce around the cauliflower. Place under the broiler (a good 10 inches away) for 4 to 5 minutes, until the sauce is bubbling and the tops of cauliflower are deeply browned/charred. Sprinkle with fresh herbs. Serve.

CHAPTER 27

When You Need Gentleness

My children and my husband treat me like a punching bag. Well, maybe a stuffed animal they love with all their might! I have, this month alone, been crashed into headfirst, punched in the derriere, taken the full weight of each of the members of my family in myriad combinations, and had pillows thrown at me. My record for saying "Gentle!" to the trinity of ruffians whom I love most in the world in a single week may well be in the triple digits. Sometimes I even try out one of my favorite lines from my favorite movies of all time, *The Aristocats,* "Because I'm a lady, that's why!"

Even in times of joy, life can be rough. Then there's the actual rough stuff: sharp words exchanged with strangers and friends alike, tragic headlines, internet schadenfreude (where some take glee in the troubles of others), and bad news clobbering our nearest and dearest.

Sometimes, when we turn to God, His mightiness can seem foreboding. Maybe a bit cold.

I'm even shocked by Jesus' own sharp tongue (um, hi, "brood of vipers," Matthew 3:7 ESV), or a move I've seen more often on *The Real Housewives of New Jersey* than at church: the flipping of the tables at the temple!

But God is a gentle giant. He is lion and lamb.

> *He will tend his flock like a shepherd; he will gather the lambs in his arms; he will carry them in his bosom, and gently lead those that are with young.*
> ISAIAH 40:11 ESV

> God is a gentle giant. He is lion and lamb.

The same God who "roars from Zion" (Joel 3:16 NASB) also gently leads the young. The one who bellows out from Jerusalem also spoke to Elijah in a gentle breeze. How can that be?

Gentleness is strength. It's a sign of towering self-control. Reminds me of watching the caress of waves lapping gently on the shore, when just a few hours earlier, the waves had lashed the sand with power and crashing. God restrains Himself with us when He knows we need a gentle touch.

The one who inspired Solomon to recognize that "a gentle answer turns away wrath" in Proverbs 15:1 NIV knows when our hearts are too bruised to receive a hard word. He made us. He sees our weakness, and He is not put off by it. When we are weak, He is strong.

We see two sides of God's personality play out in the flesh of Jesus. The Servant King defied the preconceptions of a warrior Messiah. His ministry was marked by gentleness.

You can tell a lot about someone's priorities by watching what makes them angry.

Jesus' ire was aroused at the sight of corruption, hypocrisy, spiritual legalism, and watching His loved ones suffer. I don't have many Bible verses memorized, but of course I can remember, "Jesus wept" (John 11:35). Rewind a couple of verses, and you'll see that before He wept, "a deep anger welled up within [Jesus]" (v.,33 NLT) when He saw Mary's pain over her brother Lazarus's death. He was angry at the power of death, a now-natural part of life that was not part of the original design in the Garden.

This reminds me of a common skit repeated over generations in Indian culture. When I was little, if I ran into the foot of the couch, say, my mum would calm my tears by saying, "Did the couch hurt you? Oh no! Bad couch! How dare you hurt my daughter!" And she'd feign a smack on its wooden legs. I'd instantly feel vindicated. My strong mum had shown that couch what's what!

> **He made us. He sees our weakness, and He is not put off by it.**

When we're struggling, it's not lost on Jesus just how painful life can be. The same One who will soothe our cries with His gentleness will turn around and whip the source of our pain.

Jesus empathizes with our vulnerability, because He has walked in our shoes! And He will accomplish all manner of mighty even when we only have two mites of strength to give.

But He isn't just gentle with us out of kindness. His gentleness is also our teacher. If we neglect to know the gentleness of God, we cannot emulate it! We need to grow in gentleness to foster a gentle spirit, a gentle demeanor, a gentle home. We practice it in both receiving and giving. We are gentle when we receive His gentleness.

Gentleness is God's gift to us. He extended it to us at the cross, where He put Himself on the altar, like a lamb to the slaughter. He extends it to us now, nursing us back to strength with one hand as He turns the tables with the other. He extends it to the world through us, so that His kingdom (whose banner is emblazoned with the Lion and the Lamb) will march on to glory. And so, unlike me, who can only take so much punching by my kids before I ironically roar, "GENTLE!" know that we are cared for by Jesus, whose strength is so great that He can take every fist pummeled into His chest with the strength of a lion, and yet He can be a comforting resting place for our wounded hearts with the gentleness of a lamb.

Lamb Chops with Date
and Mint Salsa

MAKES 4 SERVINGS | **TOTAL TIME**: 1 HOUR 20 MINUTES - 16 HOURS -
FOR MARINATING TIME | **ACTIVE TIME**: 35 MINUTES

8 lamb loin chops (¾ to
1-inch thick, about 2 pounds)

1 tablespoon kosher salt
(Diamond Crystal)

2 teaspoons dried mint

1½ teaspoon garam masala

½ teaspoon smoked paprika

¾ teaspoon granulated garlic

1 teaspoon dark brown sugar

Freshly ground black pepper
to taste

Avocado oil

Salsa

2 tablespoons pine nuts,
toasted

1 clove garlic, grated

8 California dates, pitted and
finely chopped (preferred:
deglet noor dates)

1½ cups mint leaves, lightly
packed

Zest of 1 Meyer lemon

6 tablespoons Meyer lemon
juice (about 1½ lemons)

6 tablespoons extra virgin
olive oil

Kosher salt + freshly ground
black pepper to taste

Aleppo pepper powder to
garnish

Hummus (either homemade,
see p. 118 or store-bought)

1. Stir together salt, dried mint, garam masala, smoked paprika, granulated garlic, brown sugar, and black pepper in a bowl. This is your spiced dry rub!

2. Using a paring knife, score the fat on the sides of the loin chops (slice in a crosshatch pattern but not deep enough to slice the meat). Now, massage the lamb chops with the rub, like you mean it! Cover with plastic wrap and refrigerate overnight. If you don't have time to do that, let them sit at room temperature for 45 minutes.

3. Make salsa, stirring together all the ingredients except for the Aleppo pepper. Taste for seasoning and set aside.

4. Preheat oven to 400 degrees Fahrenheit.

5. Heat cast iron skillet over medium-high heat. Add enough avocado oil to coat the bottom of the skillet. When it's hot enough that it shimmers, pop the chops on their sides, ie. Fat side down. lay the chops in a circle in the pan.

6. Cook for 2 minutes, then flip. Pop into the oven and cook for 12 to 15 minutes until an instant read thermometer inserted into the deepest part of the chop reads 125 degrees fahrenheit. Allow meat to rest 5 to 10 minutes.

7. Spoon the hummus onto a platter, making a well with the back of the spoon in the center. Arrange lamb chops over the hummus, drizzle salsa over the top, then sprinkle with a little extra salt and some Aleppo pepper. Serve immediately.

CHAPTER 28

When You Need Relief

Whathen I moved to Los Angeles, I took up hiking, grasping at any opportunity to breathe in something other than smog.

One day, I took a breathtaking hike along the cliffs of the Pacific Ocean. I was a bit intimated by the heights but went at my own pace, keeping my eyes out for snakes or roots, or anything else that could trip me up. Around the halfway mark, my confidence grew. I was nearly at the end, and I wasn't even tired! The Shins blared in my tinny headphones, the disc spinning in my Disc-man (oh yeah, I still had one of those), and suddenly I decided to run—downhill—over a particularly pebbly stretch. The wind streamed through my hair and my legs pumped strongly beneath me. Was this the runner's high everyone talked about?

I whizzed past other hikers, a rivulet of pride snaking its way through my heart, when all of a sudden I went flying horizontally through the air. I landed with an *oof* on my hands and knees, which immediately opened up so another river started running down my shins—not of pride but of blood. Bruised, sore, and bloody, I hobbled off the path to a tree and plopped down, panting and humbled. Today, a ghostly white patch of scar tissue on my knee reminds me that pride does indeed go before the fall.

> The only unfailing source of relief from the storm in our hearts is God.

If you're anything like me, your mind is constantly looking for trouble. It assesses any given situation for potential traps and snares, especially when my girls are with me. Our vision identifies roots on the path as we walk without our ever thinking, "Roots. Look out. Step over."

Our error-seeking mind is a splendid survival tool, but it also can be an attack dog that grabs us by the throat. It's normal to have legitimate concerns. Sadly, it's normal to have too many concerns as well.

We pride ourselves on being modern multitaskers, and yet I hope I'm not alone in feeling like there are simply too many arenas of concern at hand. I long for relief from this endless evaluation of everything.

"When I thought, 'My foot slips,' your steadfast love, O Lord, held me up. When the cares of my heart are many, your consolations cheer my soul" (Psalm 94:18–19 ESV).

> **Nothing can console our soul, nothing can refill our vital essence, like the consolations of God.**

In Hebrew, "heart" is a pretty clean swap for "mind." The psalmist observes that when our fears and evaluations of dangers multiply, it drains our vital essence, our soul! This is no small concern. This is life-threatening! Thus, when we're drowning, we can't depend on ourselves to save ourselves. We have to look elsewhere, and the only unfailing source of relief is God.

One day, my youngest daughter and I, on the hunt for an eagle's nest, had to traverse a mucky stream; the only way across was to span a slippery old log. She stood frozen, assessing the perilous path ahead of her. I held her hand.

"We'll go together," I said.

As we walked across, each time she cried out, "I'm slipping!" I grabbed her hand tighter and said, "I've got you." Gripped by fear, her spidey-senses were on high alert, interpreting every slight misstep as potential disaster. But she didn't actually need me. She was doing great! The fact that I was there helped her move through her fears, overriding her snare-seeking mind.

So too does the Lord bring relief to our minds when they are full of fears jostling against each other. We may look to a new gadget, habit, teacher, or tactic to help us when our minds are melancholy, but you and I know deep down that nothing can console our soul, nothing can refill our vital essence, like the consolations of God. And so that overrides our constantly running mind.

Because He supports us, we can rest from the endless evaluation, the perpetual high alert. Our hearts can rest knowing that even if we fail to navigate around an imminent danger, our God is there to support us. Sometimes He will carry us across the rocky path. Sometimes He will make the rough places smooth. Still other times, He will hold our hands as I held my daughter's. And while I may fall as I did on that clifftop and land with a thud on my knees, I will not fall on my face.

He is the Source of our relief. We remember Who created the path we walk on, and Who walks with us to keep us from calamity. He declares Himself as loving and supportive, our rescuer and our companion. What a delight, what a relief He is!

So let us pray one last psalm together and get cooking.

You have given me the shield of your salvation,
and your right hand supported me, and
your gentleness made me great. You gave
a wide place for my steps under me, and my feet did not slip.

PSALM 18:35-36 ESV

He is our relief.

The culinary version of relief, at least in Indian cooking, has to be Raita (RYE-tha). This yogurt-based dish sits somewhere between a condiment and a salad, and not only provides relief should you happen to eat something spicy, but also aids digestion. This one, made with pickled beets, is also gorgeous, which I think offers a specific kind of relief. A little beauty on the table can help us take a deep breath and relax!

Pickled Beet and Black Lime Raita

MAKES 4 SERVINGS | **TOTAL TIME:** 10 MINUTES | **ACTIVE TIME:** 10 MINUTES

Cook's Note: Used throughout the Middle East but particularly in the Gulf states, black lime packs a punch of sour, slightly funky flavor; it's similar to sumac. They're made by blanching then drying fresh limes in the sun. My favorite version is made by the spice company Burlap and Barrel.

1 24-ounce container whole-milk yogurt

8 ounces pickled beets, grated or thinly sliced

1 Persian cucumber, grated

Handful of pomegranate seeds, plus extra for garnish

2 to 3 tablespoons thinly sliced fresh mint, plus extra whole leaves for garnish

Kosher salt

½ teaspoon cumin seeds, toasted and ground

2 pinches of ground black lime powder or sumac (see cook's note)

Combine the yogurt, beets, cucumber, pomegranate seeds, and mint in a bowl. Season with a big pinch of salt, the cumin, and black lime. Refrigerate until ready to serve. Garnish with pomegranate seeds, mint leaves, and a little extra black lime powder.

CHAPTER 29

When You Need Comfort

I don't know about this stuff," I said to my friends as I ground fresh pepper on my favorite breakfast at my favorite diner in LA (the very recipe that accompanies this devotion). The "stuff" in question was a new-age documentary and book that was making the rounds through my circles. The DVD (remember those?) literally passed from home to home; in it, New Age luminaries looked into the camera and promised that this way of living would lead to having everything you wanted in life (wealth, prosperity, love, etc.). The key? Manifestation: envision it and then think about it constantly. You name it, you claim it. No surprise in a town where nearly everyone strove for their big break yet felt no control over how to get it, this "law of attraction" message spread like wildfire (especially amongst my friends who were all performers).

"What don't you get?" a friend asked.

I mentioned someone we knew who had just been through an unspeakable tragedy. "Are you saying that she attracted that into her life?"

> You're not crazy.
> This is hard.

Our lives are so unpredictable. One moment you're gliding through life, the next you're crashing against the mountainside. Not being able to predict what's ahead of us has haunted humanity from the beginning; we've always tried to predict or control the future, whether through fortune tellers or the power of positive thinking. I get it. The future is scary. The present hurts. We need help.

And yet, when we place the onus of our future on ourselves alone, when our solutions are all tilted toward our comfort and happiness, we actually find ourselves even more miserable. What started as a vision board of a bright, happy, prosperous future led many of my friends to self-flagellating when tragedy or disappointment struck, because according to this theory, they had called it into existence themselves.

You know what is more helpful than all of that when you just stinkin' hate your lot in life? When pain, loss, and disappointment plunge you into the depths of doldrum days? Comfort! Not change, not a new technique, not a promised golden ticket.

Comfort. Be with me, like Job's friends were:

When they saw him from a distance, they could hardly recognize him; they began to weep aloud, and they tore their robes and sprinkled dust on their heads. Then they sat on the ground with him for seven days and seven nights. No one said a word to him, because they saw how great his suffering was.

JOB 2:12-13 NIV

The Hebrew word most often used for comfort is *naham*, which connotes breathing heavily like a horse pants after exertion. It also means "to sigh." The Greek word for comfort, *parakaleo*, comes from "to call" and "alongside of," depicting a picture of someone calling out for help and another coming to their side. Sometimes the best comfort is for someone to acknowledge just how hard and painful your situation is. To suffer alongside someone, to sigh, to pant with the exertion of carrying it all, is to say, "You're not crazy. This is hard." When a solution isn't available, we comfort others with our presence, in the hopes that a burden shared would be a burden halved.

Hopefully, you have people in your life who will come and span this time with you. If you don't, or if they're taking a while to get to you, let's look at who is already sitting on the ground with us until eternity.

The Lᴏʀᴅ is near to the brokenhearted and saves the crushed in spirit.

PSALM 34:18 ESV

At the very moment when you're at your most distraught, and perhaps your loneliest, is when God is closest! Or as Charles Spurgeon put it, "Broken hearts think God is far away, when He is really most near to them; their eyes are holden so that they see not their best friend." Our grief can blind us because it's so captivating. It put blinders on our eyes so we can't see who is sitting on our right and our left.

Jesus had a similar message for His disciples:

"I have told you these things so that in me you may have peace. You will have suffering in this world. Be courageous! I have conquered the world."

JOHN 16:33 CSB

> "The Lord is near to the brokenhearted and saves the crushed in spirit."
>
> PSALM 34:18 ESV

Now, that may sound like a "buck up, chin up, put on your big girl boots, and get on with it" sort of exhortation. I want to invite you, though, to read it again with a different tone. Let's zoom out a step for context.

> *Jesus responded to them, "Do you now believe? Indeed, an hour is coming, and has come, when each of you will be scattered to his own home, and you will leave me alone. Yet I am not alone, because the Father is with me. I have told you these things so that in Me you may have peace. You will have suffering in this world. Be courageous! I have conquered the world."*
>
> JOHN 16:31-33 CSB

Unlike us, Jesus can see the future, and what He saw was not comforting. Abandoned. Betrayed. Condemned. And yet, what was the source of His comfort? His Father. God's very presence soothed His grieving heart.

Notice that Jesus didn't say that the Father would deliver Him from the imminent dangers. In fact, Jesus advised them to "be courageous," which is also sometimes translated as "be of good cheer." How in the world is that possible?

> *It is quite useless knocking at the door of heaven for earthly comfort. It's not the sort of comfort they supply there.*
>
> C. S. LEWIS

Perhaps it's that the closeness of God in our darkest hours reminds us again of just who this Yahweh is, that even this hour was written by His hand, that it was His thoughts that manifested this reality, not ours. As He wipes the tears from our eyes, we remember that He is collecting them all in a bottle. As He ushers us under His wings, we remember that He is our shield. As we begin to breathe in sync with Him, we remember that if He is with us, who can be against us?

> **As He wipes the tears from our eyes, we remember that He is collecting them all in a bottle.**

And we remember that, by the mystery of the Trinity, it isn't some distant all-powerful being that sits beside us, but Jesus, who in His humanity was so troubled by His circumstances that He sweat blood (Luke 22:44). Isn't it so much easier to take the word of someone who has been through the same trials as us?

So be of good cheer, dear one, as preposterous as that may sound. Your suffering may be great, but your Comforter is greater. His presence soothed even the blood-stained brow. He will soothe yours too.

The darker the night, the brighter the stars.
The deeper the grief, the closer is God!
FYODOR DOSTOYEVSKY

For some, when they're pained, their appetite disappears. I'm the opposite! This is a dish I reach for quite often, a reminder of my childhood when my mum would make it every few weeks. This ground beef dish is a great way to venture into Indian cooking and flavors, especially if you scoop up bites of the beef in pieces of whole wheat flatbread (*chapati*) or tortillas. Eat, dear heart. Your Comforter is by your side!

Kheema: Ground Beef with Spices and Vinegar

MAKES 4 SERVINGS | TOTAL TIME: 25 MINUTES | ACTIVE TIME: 20 MINUTES

2 pounds ground beef, 80-20

1 medium yellow onion, finely diced (about 1 cup)

8 cloves garlic, minced

1 2-inch thumb ginger, peeled and minced (about 2 tablespoons)

1 tablespoon ground coriander

2 teaspoons ground cumin

2 teaspoons paprika

1 teaspoon garam masala

½ teaspoon cayenne pepper (optional)

½ teaspoon ground turmeric

3 medium tomatoes (or canned diced fire-roasted tomatoes, drained; either way, about 1½ cups)

½ cup water

Kosher salt

1 cup frozen peas

2 teaspoon malt vinegar (or apple cider vinegar)

¼ cup chopped cilantro leaves and soft stems

1. In a large skillet over medium-high heat, add the meat. Break it up with a potato masher, season with salt, and cook until no longer pink. Remove from the skillet using slotted spoon.

2. Add the onions, season with a pinch of salt, and sauté until they're golden brown, about 5 minutes. Add the garlic and ginger, cook for another minute, stirring often.

3. Now sprinkle in ground coriander, paprika, garam masala, cumin, cayenne pepper and ground turmeric. Sauté, stirring constantly to keep the spices from burning, about 1 minute.

4. Add the beef back to the skillet, and stir well to coat every morsel with the spices.

5. Stir in tomatoes, seasoning with a pinch of salt. Cook until tomatoes start to soften.

6. Add water, stir well, cover and turn heat down to low. Cook about 10 minutes.

7. Add the peas, and cook another 5 minutes. Stir in the vinegar and chopped tomatoes. Taste for seasoning and garnish with cilantro. Serve with chapatis or whole wheat tortillas.

CHAPTER 30

When You Need to Remember

Have you forgotten your "meet cute" with Jesus?

"Meet cute" is a screenwriting term for "an amusing or charming first encounter between two characters that leads to the development of a romantic relationship between them." Remember the scene in *101 Dalmatians*, when the two humans, strangers a moment ago, get all tangled up in their dogs' leashes and soon more than fur is flying? That's a meet cute.

Meet cutes don't just need to be romantic. My first best friend, Eliana, and I bonded over making our teacher a cup of coffee every morning. (BTW, how smart was that teacher to make that a duty only the "best" kids in the class got to do?) Brendan and I met when I was walking through our dorm during New Student Week at university, and I thought, *Gosh who is playing Tori Amos so ding-dang loudly in the middle of the day?* (Hint: it was him.)

What about when your eyes were opened and you saw Jesus for exactly who He was and all the roller-coaster, all-encompassing, transformative love He had for you? Whether it's been decades or an hour, the first flush can be forgotten. We are bent to remember the negative more than the positive, and so with every heartbreaking moment of loneliness, with every ribcage-crushing moment of defeat, the dizzle-dazzle memory of the meet cute dims. It feels like a photograph; you can tell the story of the moment from memory alone, but your heart isn't in it. You can forget the uniqueness not only of the moment, but of the love of your life.

This isn't a problem unique to you or even unique in human history.

I will remember the deeds of the LORD; yes, I will remember your wonders of old.
PSALM 77:11 ESV

> "I will remember the deeds of the LORD; yes, I will remember your wonders of old."
> PSALM 77:11 ESV

No one says "I will remember" over and over again unless they know how easily they forget! You can hear the psalmist resolving to remember this thing, because this is worthy of the effort. This is important. The Hebrew word translated as remember, *zakhar*, also implies keeping it in mind. We don't remember God every now and then, when it tickles our fancy. We keep Him front of mind, much like some orthodox Jewish men wear a phylactery, a small leather box containing Scripture, on their forehead during morning prayers.

Hear, too, how the psalmist defines God's wonders "of old." The word here in Hebrew is also translated "ancient" and, curiously, "east" (we'll get to this later). The former is a good reminder that in the days before parchment was easily available, remembering was of vital importance, because once something was forgotten, it was lost forever. These days, libraries and the internet form our collective memory. We don't need to actively repeat things to ourselves in order to cement them in our memory banks. But back then there was an urgency, I imagine, to saying, "I will remember." To remember one thing was to say, *I will forget others in order to make room for this thing.*

> We don't remember God every now and then, when it tickles our fancy. We keep Him front of mind.

The ancients remembered by telling and retelling, reading and rereading aloud, singing and re-singing, the stories of how God moved amongst His people. When the sun shines and the grain is plenty, those stories can grow stale, ringing hollow in our content, complacent ears. But when all looks grim, dead on the vine, these stories we know so well can fill our dried-out hearts with as much hope and awe as they did for the original hearts in the first place.

It isn't the stories themselves that fade in meaning but our reckoning with them.

If you're having trouble remembering the last time the Holy Spirit moved so powerfully you could literally feel Him, tell the story of the time He did! What did it feel like? Try to use different words to describe it than you have in the past. What time of day was it? Fragrance is a powerful memory-recaller; what could you smell? There! Are you starting to remember?

Now try to remember (ha!) that reference to the east earlier. When we're struggling to remember our first love, perhaps it would help to face the direction from which the Son first rose in your sight. Recall the time when Jesus was just a story to you, not a divine relationship. What did you make of Jesus of Nazareth? What changed? How did He break through the wall of unbelief? How did you change as a result of His love?

Isaiah calls Christians "ye that are Yahweh's remembrancers" (Isaiah 62:6 ASV). This is a two-toned word, meaning that we remind God of our needs, but also that we remember Him and His ways. Over the centuries, our spiritual forefathers and foremothers wrote His words down, built altars to remember what He had done for them in that place, and composed songs about how He had rescued them. Ritual and sacrament were created in obedience to Jesus, who asked that we do these things in remembrance of Him. Art, literature, and music are built on the foundation of His stories. We

We are God's remembrancers.

choose to remember, because left to our own devices, we are naturally people for whom the stories dim. We are people who forget, but because of Christ, we resolve to be different. We are God's remembrancers.

Throughout my life, whether it has been great victories or tragedies, I have always turned to food to either celebrate or soothe. My favorite food for either the peak or the valley? Ice cream! These ice cream sandwiches are a remembrance of the gift of my family: Rose and Marigold are the middle names of our girls, the result of Brendan and I meeting all those many years ago.

As you make these ice cream sandwiches, try to remember your meet cute with Jesus. Where were you? How did it feel? Maybe it's time to ask God to fill you with His Spirit again. Talk to Him as you crumble, chop, and scoop.

Rose and Marigold Ice Cream Sandwiches with Saffron Ice cream

MAKES 4 SERVINGS | **TOTAL TIME:** 35 MINUTES | **ACTIVE TIME:** 15 MINUTES

Cook's Note: Pizzelle are thin waffle cookies from Italy. You can find them at finer supermarkets or online. I love the anise flavor but if you're not a licorice fan, you might prefer the vanilla!

2 tablespoons warm milk

2 big pinches saffron threads

1 pint good quality vanilla ice cream

¼ cup dried rose petals

¼ cup dried marigold or calendula petals

¼ cup toasted, coarsely chopped pistachios

8 pizzelle (anise or vanilla flavor; see Cook's Note)

1. Gently crumble saffron threads between your fingers and sprinkle into warm milk. Cover and allow to steep for 20 minutes. Set ice cream out at room temperature to soften.

2. Either chop by hand or use a small food processor to cut rose petals down to a coarse powder. Pour onto a plate. Repeat with the marigold petals.

3. Scoop ice cream out into a bowl, and fold in saffron milk and finely chopped pistachios with a spatula. Place back in the freezer for 15 minutes to firm up.

4. Set a piece of parchment paper onto a sheet pan, and clear room in your freezer for it!

5. Spread ¼ of the ice cream (about ½ cup) across a pizzelle, from edge to edge, to a ½-inch thickness. Top with another pizzelle and gently squeeze so ice cream oozes out the sides. Quickly roll in rose and marigold petals. Set on prepared baking sheet, and repeat with remaining pizzelles and ice cream. Either serve immediately or freeze until ice cream firms, making it easy to slice into wedges.

When You Need Something Special

CHAPTER 31

When You Need Abundance

Do you know what the largest living thing on the planet is? It's not an elephant or a blue whale. Nope. It's a mushroom.

The humongous fungus, to be exact (I'm not kidding), a single fungal organism found in the Malheur National Forest in Oregon. It covers three and a half square miles. The most extraordinary thing? Were you to walk across it, you probably wouldn't even notice it.

The main body of the fungus exists underground, where a complex network of fibers called mycelium feast on soil and decomposing material. When it's time to make more humongous funguses, you'll see wee mushrooms popping up on the forest floor. Each mushroom is part of the same organism, even though it's miles from its doppelgänger.

What does this have to do with abundance?!

You've heard the sermon. We've heard it on the radio, while sitting in the pew, on TV. "If you give today, Jesus will reward you many times over!"

The message on biblical abundance has been twisted many times over. Like me, I'm sure you've watched loved ones (maybe yourself), in an hour of desperation, give in to bad shepherds. Frankly, prosperity preachers who teach more on material prosperity than spiritual prosperity kept me from talking to God about my own needs for a long time. I walked away from what looked like a rotting cluster of fungus . . . but was really a treasure chest underneath. And that's a tragedy.

> When we bring our possessions to the altar—this simple act burns away at our need for those things.

Abundance is defined as having "more than enough." By contrast, Jesus owned just the robes on His back and the sandals on His feet. And yet I think of people like Lydia, the successful businesswoman who used her wealth to build up the early church. God clearly doesn't hold back material blessings from some of His children. So what does He actually say about the abundant life?

"Bring the full tithe into the storehouse, that there may be food in my house.
And thereby put me to the test, says the LORD of hosts,
if I will not open the windows of heaven for you and
pour down for you a blessing until there is no more need."

MALACHI 3:10 ESV

This is true of money. This is true of attention. This is true of time, effort, will, our desire, our heart. Give what God has asked for, and He will return it manifold. As far as I can tell, the pathway to abundance in our lives follows a tried-and-true path.

First: sacrifice, a willingness to surrender all we have.

It's no wonder we take so much security in our possessions; they keep fear, anxiety, perhaps even danger at bay! But when we bring them to the altar, the simple act of doing so burns away at our need for those things. Our attachment to those things weakens. This is the blessing God pours down from the windows of heaven: "there will be no more need," either because He fills that need or because He eliminates our desire for that need altogether. Where we once tasted a temporary peace, now we taste emancipation in the form of a deeper attachment to the Giver, the Source of true peace. Surrender upon surrender leads to freedom upon freedom. And freedom tastes an awful lot like abundance, doesn't it?

> Surrender upon surrender leads to freedom upon freedom.

Where God asked for one-tenth of the harvest as a tithe, Jesus pushes even more. "Sell all that you have" (Matthew 19:21; Luke 18:22)! His point: you can give up everything you own and still have abundance. What is He talking about?

We often ask God for abundance when drought strikes. Scarcity makes us stockpile with a white-knuckled grip. But Jesus does the opposite. Where we put ourselves first and hoard, He puts Himself last and gives.

"The thief comes only to steal and kill and destroy.
I came that they may have life and have it abundantly."

JOHN 10:10 ESV

Even if our storehouses may not be abundant, in Him we have more than enough. He is abundance personified. And He has given Himself to us. Abundance makes its dwelling place within us! We could lose it all, be in the midst of nothing but chaos, and He is there with us.

Think of the mushrooms popping up in the Oregon woods; those cheery but piddly puffs aren't the evidence of the vast, powerful network that lies beneath. No! You must dig past the surface to find the riches beneath.

In Him we have more than enough.

So, you need abundance? Start with gratitude for what you have and confidence in the Provider, not the provision. And then give! And when you do, imagine that resource attached to the mycelium of abundance from which it was given to you. It wasn't yours to hold onto. It's yours to give, because He who is the source of all abundance in the universe lives in you.

Now to him who is able to do far more abundantly than all that we ask or think, according to the power at work within us, to him be glory in the church and in Christ Jesus throughout all generations, forever and ever. Amen.
EPHESIANS 3:20-21 ESV

There are lots of different kinds of abundance we "need" in our daily lives; money, time, and health to name a few. Imagine putting the one that's most front of mind on the altar now. Think through your wish list: If I could give that back to you, in triplicate, what would you expend that abundance on? Then, next to each thing you list, write down what need it meets.

For example, for me, if I could be gifted the four hours I tithed to my church, I would use it to clean the house properly. The need that would be met is my peace.

Then, together, let's access the vast network available to us, hidden in Christ. Let's go to our Provider and ask for abundance above and beyond! Amen.

Dimsum Stuffed Mushrooms

MAKES 24 STUFFED MUSHROOMS | TOTAL TIME: 1 HOUR 30 MINUTES | ACTIVE TIME: 1 HOUR

24 large stuffing mushrooms, wiped clean with damp paper towel, stems and gills removed

2 tablespoons avocado or other neutral flavored oil

½ pound ground pork

1 tablespoon Shaoxing rice wine

½ teaspoon sesame oil

¾ teaspoon white granulated sugar

1 teaspoon cornstarch

1 tablespoon soy sauce

1 tablespoon grated ginger

3 scallions, white and green parts minced

⅛ teaspoon white pepper

Kosher salt and freshly ground black pepper

Dipping Sauce

1 tablespoon soy sauce

3 tablespoons Chinese black vinegar (or substitute 1½ tablespoons malt vinegar plus 1½ tablespoons unseasoned rice wine vinegar)

1. Preheat the oven to 425 degrees Fahrenheit. Ensure oven rack is in middle position. Line a sheet with parchment paper or foil.

2. In a large bowl, gently toss mushroom caps with 2 tablespoons oil. Season with salt and freshly ground black pepper. Now lay the mushrooms, gill-side up, on the sheet pan. Roast for 20 minutes. The mushrooms will be full of water. Tip them upside down, and roast for another 10 minutes until well browned. Remove from the oven. Turn heat up to 450 degrees Fahrenheit.

3. Place ground pork in a large bowl. With clean hands, mix Shaoxing wine, sesame oil, sugar, cornstarch, soy sauce, grated ginger, and most of the scallions (leave some for garnish!), white pepper, a pinch of salt and a few grinds of black pepper, until well combined but not over-mixed.

4. Spoon 1 to 2 teaspoons of ground pork mixture into each mushroom depending on the size of the opening. Pop back into the oven and bake for 15 minutes until pork is cooked through. Remove from oven and allow to cool for 5 minutes.

5. Stir soy sauce and black vinegar together to make dipping sauce.

6. Sprinkle mushrooms with reserved scallions and serve with the dipping sauce immediately!

CHAPTER 32

When You Need Healing

My husband, Brendan, has been helping me write these devotionals. I fell behind, and being a lover of God, me, and the Bible, he sprang into action, writing down his thoughts on some of these entries. As you may know, Bren suffers from a disease called ulcerative colitis. He had it once before when he was very young, and the Lord healed him in a way the doctors couldn't explain. We are waiting on God to do it again. I figured in this instance I'd leave Bren's words just as they are, because if you're seeking healing, who better to hear from than someone else doing the same.

Come, let us return to the LORD. He has torn us to pieces but He will heal us; He has injured us but He will bind up our wounds. After two days He will revive us; on the third day He will restore us, that we may live in His presence.
HOSEA 6:1-2 NIV

Lepers, evildoers, the stone hearted, and spiritually dead, Jesus' ministry was replete with healing. It was revival deluxe! Every single eyewitness account that comprises the Gospels mentions Jesus performing miracles of healing. These miracles are a special testimony to Jesus' nature; not only did He have access to the power to heal, but His motivation to heal was love.

Therefore many other signs Jesus also performed in the presence of the disciples, which are not written in this book; but these have been written so that you may believe that Jesus is the Christ, the Son of God; and that by believing you may have life in His name.
JOHN 20:30-31 NASB

We have life in His name. But this life is still filled with suffering, suffering from which He can heal but suffering He doesn't always perform miracles to heal.

"I have told you these things, so that in Me you may have [perfect] peace. In the world you have tribulation and distress and suffering, but be courageous [be confident, be undaunted, be filled with joy]; I have overcome the world. [My conquest is accomplished, My victory abiding.]"
JOHN 16:33 AMP

I'll totally admit that I don't always like it. But it is true. And yes, of course, I understand how it can start to seem like a cop-out. Like a "You know that thing I promised you? Yes! I will . . . not exactly give you that but I will heal the part of you that thinks it needs that."

We have life in His name.

Here we get to wrestling, don't we? Way too often, we feel ashamed when we feel like we're really tussling with God.

You know what? He ain't scared of no tussle! This is Jehovah we're talking about! This is God, who named His people, Israel, "he who wrestles with God." Our Father is not worried about our wrestling moves.

So come on, let's wrestle! Yes, we know we are being healed of discontent even as our bodies may continue to be ravaged.

"Not that I am speaking of being in need, for I have learned in whatever situation I am to be content" (Philippians 4:11 ESV).

Yes, we know that we are healed of the pride of life (doing everything in our own strength) by the abiding grace of God, even as our souls are drained so rapidly it feels like we're bleeding out.

"My grace is sufficient for you, for my power is made perfect in weakness." Therefore I will boast all the more gladly of my weaknesses, so that the power of Christ may rest upon me.
II CORINTHIANS 12:9 ESV

Yes, we know that in our infirmity, He is calling us to draw deeper into community, into asking not only Jehovah Jireh, our Provider, for healing but also asking others.

Is anyone among you suffering? Let him pray. Is anyone cheerful? Let him sing praise. Is anyone among you sick? Let him call for the elders of the church, and let them pray over him, anointing him with oil in the name of the Lord. And the prayer of faith will save the one who is sick, and the Lord will raise him up. And if he has committed sins, he will be forgiven.
JAMES 5:13-15 ESV

Yes Lord. Yes, children of God! We know all that.

But . . . we also just want to be healed. We'll take the character development and the depths of understanding and the transformative divine family later. We really want to be healed. Our faith is strong. Our flesh is weak. We've asked. We've pleaded. We've been anointed with olive oil from a tourist trap in Jerusalem, with avocado oil from Costco, with the oil of our tears and the tears of our loved ones and . . . we still are not healed.

Yes, the many comforts God promises are precious. I want you to know, though, beloved, when the riches of His love don't seem like they're enough, and even when we know we're wrong in our estimation of our present situation . . . you can keep coming back to the feet of the Lamb not only to kiss them in gratitude, but to also invite Him to a wrestling match.

> When the riches of His love don't seem like they're enough, you can keep coming back to the feet of the Lamb.

He will not flee from you in disgust. He will not have a referee stop the fight. He will never leave you or forsake you, even in this. Even when you're too tired to wrestle Him anymore. He will hold you. He will.

Tomorrow we'll rise and pray again, like a prophet of old who cursed his own birth more than once:

> *Heal me, O Lᴏʀᴅ, and I shall be healed;*
> *save me, and I shall be saved, for you are my praise.*
> JEREMIAH 17:14 ESV

While you're making piccata, pray for healing. Think about who in your community you can call on for healing. Your elders. Your family. Your friends. Pray again. See what God can do. Never stop wrestling.

Between the assertive lemony zip and the strong salty pop of capers in this dish, I've always felt a little brighter, a little more energetic after a plate of piccata, which is why I thought it appropriate for a meditation on healing. Maybe it's all the vitamin C! In this version, I added the Middle Eastern spice za'atar, which adds an herbal, sour punch to the dish that feels quite at home. There's something about citrus and herbs that always feels right when I'm not feeling well, and even if it doesn't actually heal my bones, it always brightens my outlook.

Za'atar Piccata

MAKES 2 TO 3 SERVINGS | **TOTAL TIME:** 40 TO 45 MINUTES | **ACTIVE TIME:** 40 TO 45 MINUTES

1½ pounds boneless skinless chicken breasts (2 to 4)

½ cup all-purpose flour

3 tablespoons za'atar, divided

5 tablespoons extra virgin olive oil, divided

4 tablespoons unsalted butter, divided

1 shallot, minced

1 clove garlic, minced

½ cup low-sodium chicken broth

⅛ teaspoon ground turmeric

2 tablespoons fresh lemon juice

¼ cup capers, drained

2 tablespoons chopped parsley

Kosher salt and freshly ground black pepper

1. Make chicken cutlets by halving them horizontally. Each slice should be ¼-inch thick. If they aren't, place between two sheets of plastic wrap, and pound with a meat pounder or a heavy pan until they're the correct thickness.

2. In a shallow dish, stir together flour, 2 tablespoons za'atar, 1 teaspoon kosher salt, and a few grinds of freshly ground black pepper. Season chicken cutlets with salt and pepper. Dredge them thoroughly in the flour mixture, shaking gently to remove excess. Place on wire rack in baking sheet.

3. Heat ¼ cup olive oil and 2 tablespoons butter in 12-inch skillet over medium-high heat until just starting to smoke. Add half the chicken pieces, leaving plenty of room between them. Brown well on each side, about 5 to 6 minutes total. Remove to a plate and repeat with remaining chicken.

4. Add remaining 1 tablespoon olive oil to the pan, add shallots and garlic, and cook until softened. Add broth, turmeric, remaining 1 tablespoon za'atar, and lemon juice to the pan. Bring to a simmer.

5. Add chicken cutlets to the sauce, and simmer for 2 minutes, flipping halfway through. Transfer cutlets to serving platter. Sauce should be consistency of heavy cream. If not, simmer for another minute or so.

6. Off heat, whisk in last 2 tablespoons of butter. Stir in capers and parsley. Taste for seasoning, adding salt, pepper, and lemon juice as needed. Spoon sauce over chicken and serve!

CHAPTER 33

When You Need Provision

Then Jesus said to His disciples, "Therefore I tell you, do not worry about your life, what you will eat; or about your body, what you will wear. For life is more than food, and the body more than clothes. Consider the ravens: They do not sow or reap, they have no storehouse or barn; yet God feeds them. How much more valuable you are than the birds! Who of you by worrying can add a single hour to your life? So if you cannot do such a small thing, why do you worry about the rest? Consider how the lilies grow: They do not labor or spin. Yet I tell you, not even Solomon in all his glory was dressed like one of these. If that is how God clothes the grass of the field, which is here today and tomorrow is thrown into the fire, how much more will He clothe you—you of little faith! And do not set your heart on what you will eat or drink; do not worry about it. For the pagan runs after such these things, and your Father knows that you need them. But seek His kingdom, and these things will be added to you as well."

LUKE 12:22-31 NIV

Okay, done here! Right? Cool? Do you feel better now? Great! This was a short one. Let's get cooking!

"Wait!"

That would have been me had I been in the audience that day. One arm up in the air, finger pointing to the sky. "I have follow-up questions!"

And maybe He would have smiled wearily, knowing what I was about to ask.

"All due respect, Rabbi, but you're a single man with no children. You're fed by others wherever you go! I've got kids and a husband and parents to feed! We live in the desert so water is definitely a concern. Plus there's Roman soldiers and tax collectors and high priests breathing down my neck! It's a lot!! Don't be concerned? Don't you think that's a bit . . . easy for you to say?" I'd say, wincing at the end there.

> "I have some questions."

Okay, maybe I wouldn't have. I'm polite, to a fault. Maybe I'd have waited until after His sermon and the chaotic queue of evildoers and lepers and undercover Pharisees died down and said, "I have some questions."

Because I do have questions. On the one hand I know Jesus doesn't lie. And yet . . . I don't feel settled. I don't always feel provided for. Like most women, not only am I a wife and mother and business-builder, but I'm also the house manager, scanning the horizon for upcoming bills, needs, and potential dearth. I read the headlines like tea leaves, trying to figure out what's coming. I make adjustments to our spending depending on what the headlines reveal. I scan the sales when I foresee the girls need for swimsuits. There's a running list in my head at all times of everyone in my household's needs and a simultaneous list of which of those we can fill and which we cannot (the latter is always longer).

To be even more honest, I sometimes think that God provides me things I do not want more often than I'd prefer. Another job? Hooray! Thank You, Father! Another job where I have to do something that scares the you-know-what out of me and sends me into imposter syndrome spirals? No thanks!

In my head, of course, I believe Him, I take Him at His word. But in my belly, where my fear lies, doubt festers. Does He really mean it? This teaching of Jesus sometimes makes me jealous of the ravens, covetous of the lilies. Oh, the simplicity! The ease of not caring, with no running list, no analysis of the horizon. Just searching or waiting and finding what you need . . . Wait a second.

Maybe that's the key. Provision is coming because not only was it promised, but it was also promised by the One who never breaks promises.

> **Provision is coming because not only was it promised, but it was also promised by the One who never breaks promises.**

The ravens aren't fed because they're gauging rising bird seed prices and buying in bulk while they're low. The lilies aren't resplendently attired because they design and sow into the wee hours. Hustle culture, boss lady attitudes, and my nonstop worrying aren't adding any more hours to my family's lives than God has already assigned. I'm provided for simply because He loves me and He said He would. It's as simple as that.

And perhaps that's when Jesus would nod at me and say, "Yup. You get it."

Maybe I'd smile sheepishly. Mayhaps He'd ask if my mum was cooking that night, and I'd say yes, and brag on her excellent kofta kebabs, to which He'd raise an eyebrow and I'd panic and say, "but I don't think she's making enough for thirteen extra guests!"

And He'd raise the other eyebrow.

"Oh she is? Mmmmmm, I don't think you know my mum because she . . . Oh wait, this is another one of those trust moments, isn't it? Okay. Let's go."

And I'd walk Him and the disciples to our house and treat them to a feast because I'm guessing we'd just so happen to have just enough lamb kebabs and salad to feed us all, full to the brim, with plenty of leftovers.

I'm provided for simply because He loves me and He said He would. It's as simple as that.

Kefta Kebabs with Pomegranate Grain Salad

MAKES 16 KEBABS, ABOUT 8 SERVINGS | **TOTAL TIME:** 45 MINUTES TO 1 HOUR
ACTIVE TIME: 45 MINUTES TO 1 HOUR

Kebabs

1 medium yellow onion (250g), coarsely chopped

2 cloves garlic, chopped

½ cup parsley leaves

1 pound ground lamb

1 pound ground beef

1 tablespoon baharat or garam masala

1 teaspoon sumac

1 teaspoon pomegranate molasses

1 teaspoon kosher salt

½ teaspoon black pepper

1 teaspoon baking soda

Avocado oil for cooking

Pomegranate grain salad

2 tablespoons lemon juice (from 1 to 2 lemons)

2 tablespoons extra virgin olive oil

½ teaspoon pomegranate molasses

1 ½ cups cooked freekeh, farro, quinoa or brown rice, cooled to room temperature

1 cup fresh pomegranate seeds (arils)

1½ cups finely chopped parsley, about 1 bunch

¾ cup finely chopped mint leaves, about 1 bunch

Kosher salt and freshly ground black pepper

Tahini sauce

¼ cup tahini

2 tablespoons lemon juice (from 1 to 2 lemons)

2 tablespoons olive oil

¼ cup hot water, plus more as needed

1. Soak 32 wooden skewers in cool water for 30 minutes.

2. In a food processor, pulse onion, garlic, and parsley until finely minced. Add ground lamb and beef, baharat or garam masala, sumac, pomegranate molasses, kosher salt, black pepper, and baking soda. Process until well combined paste forms, scraping down sides to ensure even blending. Scoop out of the food processor into a large bowl.

3. Form kebabs: fill a small bowl with cool water. Lightly oil a sheet pan. Dip your hands into the water, to keep the meat from sticking to you, and divide

meat mixture into 16 portions, forming each into a ball. Roll one into a 4-inch log, then thread skewer through its length. Run another skewer alongside it. Now, form meat into a somewhat flat, 6- to 7-inch-long kebab, rectangular in shape. Skewer ball, then shape into a 6- to 7- inch-long cyclinder, about ½-inch in diameter. Transfer to sheet pan, and repeat with remaining mixture. Refrigerate while you make the salad at the sauce.

4. Make salad: whisk together lemon juice, extra virgin olive oil, and pomegranate molasses along with a hefty pinch of salt and pepper in a large bowl. Now add freekeh, pomegranate seeds, parsley, and mint. Toss together gently. Taste for seasoning and adjust accordingly.

5. Make tahini sauce: In a medium bowl, whisk together tahini, lemon juice, olive oil, and hot water, seasoning with salt and pepper. If sauce is too thick, add more hot water, until sauce is luxuriously creamy. Set aside.

6. Heat cast iron griddle over medium high heat. Drizzle kebabs with a little avocado oil. Spray griddle with avocado oil spray. Lay kebabs on griddle, cooking about 8 at a time. Cook without moving until meat easily releases from pan, about 2 minutes. Flip and continue to cook until well browned, and meat registers 160 degrees Fahrenheit, about 8 minutes total. Transfer to a large platter with tahini sauce and pomegranate salad. Serve.

CHAPTER 34

When You Need Wisdom

Do you remember the old Tootsie Pop commercial?

It opens on a boy holding a lollipop with a hard candy shell, containing a chewy chocolate center. He approaches a turtle with the question burning in the consciousness of every child: "How many licks does it take to get to the Tootsie Roll center of a Tootsie Pop?"

The turtle says he doesn't know because he can never stop biting before he's discovered the answer. The boy finds an owl, bedecked in a scholarly hat, and asks the same question.

The owl takes the lollipop from the boy and says, "Let's find out." He licks it.

"One." He licks again.

"Two." Once more.

"Three," he says, rolling the *R*.

Then he bites into the lollipop with a loud crunch and hands it back to the chagrined boy.

"Three," he pronounces definitively.

"How many licks does it take to get to the Tootsie Roll center of a Tootsie Pop?" intones a baritone announcer guy. "The world may never know."

> **Fearing the Lord equals wisdom.**

When I need wisdom, I'm as impatient as that owl. I need to get to the center ASAP! As a daughter of God, I know I'm not to lean on my own understanding. So, where should I go for wisdom?

> *The fear of the Lord is the beginning of wisdom, and*
> *knowledge of the Holy One is understanding.*
> PROVERBS 9:10 NIV

This premise is foundational to gaining wisdom. Fearing the Lord equals wisdom. The "fear" here is honor and respect, knowing He's high up on that branch above you with His scholar's cap affixed.

It's also straight up fear! Remember the reaction of the disciples after Jesus calmed the storm? It wasn't relief. It was fear! Of Him! Who is this man who can control even the winds? If He can do that to the storm, honestly, what could He do to me?

We don't like to talk about this, especially because it might discourage those considering joining us on The Way, but I find this to be true: to be in awe of something necessitates being a little terrified when you think on it too long! Consider the deafening roar of a mighty waterfall or the cold sweat that develops when you stare into the eyes of a lion through the bars at the zoo. To know God is to experience that same combination of joy and cold sweats!

Fear and love don't cancel each other out here. Rather they clarify the positions of who we are in this love relationship.

> The more time we spend at His feet, the more we understand His ways, the more we can apply that understanding.

Knowledge is relational at its core. If it were a Tootsie Pop, your relationship with God would be at the center of it, so much so that the same word in Hebrew can be translated "devotion." The more time we spend at His feet, the more we understand His ways and His thinking . . . the more we understand, the more we can apply that understanding to the chaos of our lives. Wisdom is active, the application of the understanding we've acquired by knowing God.

I like flow charts, so here's the pathway to wisdom, as best as I can figure it out:

Devotion –> Knowledge of God –> Understanding God while also fearing Him –> Applying understanding to our lives (aka, wisdom)!

So perhaps that's why James, the brother of Jesus (can you imagine their relationship?), encouraged us to take the path of least resistance when we need wisdom:

> If any of you lacks wisdom, let him ask God, who gives generously
> to all without reproach, and it will be given him.
>
> JAMES 1:5 ESV

Is it just that easy? Yes! Even the act of asking for wisdom is in itself an act of wisdom, because it's building on your relationship with Wisdom Himself. Expect to receive it . . . over the long term. God's wisdom is not gained by biting straight through to the center. No, it's accrued over a lifetime of going to the source: tasting and digesting each layer, which gives away to another one, until finally we arrive at the center, which

I suggest may lie just beyond the pearly gates, when all will truly be revealed and we will see Wisdom face to face! Hallelujah!

Here's an idea. Set a timer for ten minutes and find a quiet spot, even if it's in the bathroom! Sit with Wisdom. Ask Him to bless you with more.

I don't have a recipe for Tootsie Rolls, but here's one for these luscious chocolate cakes that have just a little fudge in the center. Think of that center as your relationship with God—your devotion to Him. As you cook these chocolate cakes, reflect on anything you learned or experienced in your devotion time with Him earlier. Any nuggets of wisdom?

> **Wisdom is active, the application of the understanding we've acquired by knowing God.**

Flourless Chocolate Cakes

MAKES 12 SERVINGS | **TOTAL TIME:** 1 HOUR 5 MINUTES | **ACTIVE TIME:** 30 MINUTES

1 stick (4 ounces) unsalted butter, plus extra softened butter for greasing pans

6 ounces (176g) bittersweet chocolate (not chocolate chips)

Unsweetened cocoa for dusting

2 large eggs, at room temperature

2 large egg yolks, at room temperature

¼ cup (65g) granulated cane sugar

7 tablespoons tahini

Creme fraiche or whipped cream to serve.

Halvah or toasted sesame seeds to garnish

Zest of 1 lime

Flaky salt

1. Preheat oven to 350 degrees Fahrenheit.

2. Set a heatproof bowl over a saucepan of gently simmering water. Make sure the bottom of the bowl isn't touching the water. Add stick of butter and chocolate, breaking the latter into pieces. Stir mixture together until just melted and smooth. Remove from heat and set aside.

3. Use extra butter to grease a 12-cup muffin tin. Dust with cocoa (I like to use a tea strainer). Set aside.

4. Using a stand mixer with a whisk attachment, beat the eggs, egg yolks, sugar, and a pinch of salt on medium-low speed, until thickened and pale, about 3 to 4 minutes.

5. Gently whisk in the tahini and cooled chocolate. Using an ice cream scoop, add mixture to the prepared muffin tin, and bake for 10 to 12 minutes, until sides of cake are firm but centers are soft. Allow the cakes to cool for 10 minutes before serving. Serve each cake with a dollop of creme fraiche, and finish with a sprinkle of halvah, lime zest, and flake salt.

CHAPTER 35

When You Need Satisfaction

Fat. Relationship Status: It's Complicated.

When I was about eight years old, we went to London for our summer holidays to visit my great-uncle Wilfie and great-aunty Milla.

Uncle Wilfie was a giant, truly, with heavy eyebrows and a voice so deep that it made my bones hum in my chest. And yet, he was also one of the gentlest, kindest people I'd ever met. A chubby child, I hated our shopping trips in London. My younger sister, slender as a fox, looked wonderful in everything she tried on. She never had trouble finding her size. The waistbands didn't cut into her skin. Aka the opposite of me.

One evening, upon returning after a day of humilia–, I mean, shopping, Uncle Wilfie noticed my downcast spirit.

"Aarti, darling, you're not fat. You're pleasantly plump!"

I smiled. He chuckled. For a moment, that simple phrase satisfied my longing to be seen as lovely.

Like so many, I have a complicated relationship with fat. As a human being with a capacity for pleasure, I like fat. As a human being who suffers from body dysmorphia, I hate it. On me. I'm grateful for the era of body positivity so my daughters won't grow up with quite the same weight obsession I did.

> That simple phrase satisfied my longing to be seen as lovely.

Fat is vital to any dish. Ghee is foundational to more dishes than I could name in Indian cooking. Butter is an essential element to American cuisine. Fat is not only flavorful in and of itself, but it also allows flavor compounds to be detected, which is why we bloom spices in fat to get the most flavor out of them. Fat makes things crispy or creamy, silky or sumptuous. It adds a glossy sheen that should be its own Instagram filter by now. This is satisfaction to our eyes, to our tongue, to our palate.

Did you know our brain is 70 percent fat? So fat provides literal building blocks for our ability to think and thrive. Healthy fats foster a healthy "second brain" (the gut), which among other things fosters a healthy microbiome and produces a satiety response in our intestines. Good fat makes my body, soul, and mind function in satisfying fashion.

So, what satisfies our soul? So often, it can feel like we're back-up singers to Mick Jagger: "I can't get no . . . satisfaction!"

Fat is complicated because we complicate it. Satisfaction is complicated because we complicate it.

> *God, You are my God; I shall be watching for You;*
> *My soul thirsts for You, my flesh yearns for You,*
> *In a dry and exhausted land where there is no water.*
> *So have I seen You in the sanctuary,*
> *To see Your power and glory.*
> *Because Your favor is better than life,*
> *My lips will praise You. So I will bless You as long as I live;*
> *I will lift up my hands in Your name.*
> *My soul is satisfied as with fat and fatness,*
> *And my mouth offers praises with joyful lips.*
> PSALM 63:1-5 NASB

The psalmist likens the satisfaction of fat to his tongue and his body to the satisfaction of his relationship with the Father. Not only does it produce joy by hitting his pleasure sensors, but it's also nourishing to his body. Right relationship with God tastes good . . . like a piece of fried chicken, like cumin seeds and onions sizzled in ghee, like a knob of bone marrow (aka meat butter) on a piece of toast.

Just as we're created to yearn for fat, we're created with a longing for God!

We may seek satisfaction all over creation, but it's a satisfaction that only the Creator can provide. Once we've tasted and seen that the Lord is good, everything else feels like "a dry and exhausted land where there is no water." The psalmist is spoiled, having seen God in the sanctuary, much like, once you have had great full-fat ice cream, you can't eat the low-fat stuff anymore. It just doesn't satisfy in the same way.

Right relationship with God tastes good.

"What is it then that this desire and this inability proclaim to us, but that there was once in man a true happiness of which there now remains to him only; the mark and the empty trace, which he in vain tried to fill from all his surroundings, seeking from things absent the help he does not obtain in things present? But these are all inadequate, because the infinite abyss can only be filled by an infinite and immutable Object, that is to say, only by God Himself" (Blaise Pascal).

Let this be an encouragement to your soul, dear one. While we might have a complicated relationship with fat, with satisfaction, with God Himself . . . He does not. In Christ, God is satisfied with you! Jesus' sacrifice on the cross means that He looks at you through the perfect, flawless veil of Christ, in Whom He is well pleased, aka, more than satisfied. If God is satisfied with us, what satisfaction could we find elsewhere? What could be better? It's sort of how Uncle Wilfie saw me. While I saw all my flaws and ugliness, what he saw made him smile with pride and glee. So does our Father gaze upon us!

> We may seek satisfaction all over creation, but it's a satisfaction that only the Creator can provide.

So yes, my relationship with fat remains complicated. But my relationship with God is meant to be uncomplicated, one of life's simple yet oh so satisfying joys. It's like eating some good fat without any of the complications I confound it with. My body, mind, and soul yearn for Him. And good news! I can have as much of Him as I want! He is never-ending! Now, that's not so complicated, is it?

When I think of satisfying fats, the most decadent of them has to be bone marrow, which some chefs call "meat butter"! I used to think it was a difficult dish to prepare, but it requires nothing more than soaking and roasting. Savor every bite. Feel the satisfaction of the fat hitting your tongue, balanced by the bright zing of the salad. Don't complicate it. Just enjoy it. It's good.

Bone Marrow with Green Apple Kachumber

MAKES 4 TO 6 SERVINGS | **TOTAL TIME:** 12 HR 25 MINUTES TO 24 HR 25 MINUTES | **ACTIVE TIME:** 25 MINUTES

Cook's Note: Kachumber is a South Asian salad that lends freshness to rich curries, which is why it's a perfect companion to the richness of bone marrow. Ask your butcher to slice your marrow bones lengthwise for the best presentation, but if you can only find bones that are cut crosswise, those will work too. Ask for center-cut bones; they have the most marrow. You don't have to soak the bones before cooking but it will make for a prettier dish because it removes blood and impurities. I'm guessing there's a metaphor there but I'll let you figure that one out!

4 3-inch beef marrow bones, sliced lengthwise (see Cook's Note)

Kosher salt

Toasted slices of good bread

Kachumber

1 tablespoon lemon juice, about ¼ lemon

¼ teaspoon chaat masala (optional)

¼ teaspoon cumin seeds, toasted and coarsely ground in a mortar and pestle

1 small shallot, thinly sliced

1 cup cilantro leaves, soft stems minced

½ cup peeled green apple, cut into ¼ inch dice (about ½ medium apple)

Freshly ground black pepper

Flaked salt

1. Fill a large bowl halfway up with ice water, and dissolve salt in the water using a proportion of 1 teaspoon salt to 1 cup water. Add marrow bones, and refrigerate for 12 to 24 hours, changing out the salty water every 4 hours.

2. Drain bones, and pat dry. Preheat oven to 450 degrees Fahrenheit.

3. Make the salad: Whisk together lemon juice, chaat masala (if using), and cumin together with a good pinch of salt. Stir in shallots, and allow to sit for 5 minutes. Add cilantro leaves, apple, and a few grinds of black pepper, tossing to coat well.

4. Line a sheet pan or roasting pan with parchment paper. Arrange marrow bones cut side up. If cut crosswise, place wider end on the bottom. Roast bones for 15 to 20 minutes until marrow has puffed up and the center registers 145 degrees Fahrenheit. Remove from the oven.

5. To serve, sprinkle marrow bones with a little flaky salt. Serve kachumber either on the side or spooned over the top of the bones. Place a few pickled mustard seeds over the top too. Serve with toasted bread. To eat, scoop out some bone marrow, along with the kachumber, and smear on a piece of toast. Eat, enjoy, and be satisfied!

CHAPTER 36

When You Need Someone to Listen

One of the keys to making great pulao, or pilaf, is to listen. Once you add the soaked and drained rice to the aromatic fat, you must lend those grains your ears! The last droplets of water that cling to the grains will transform to vapor, allowing the starches to start to caramelize in the fat. When that happens, the music in your pot will change from a wet sssshhhhhhhh to the snappy staccato of a sizzle. The loamy gentle scent of basmati rice changes to a toasty nuttiness. Then and only then will we add the liquid. Cooking the tastiest pilaf on the planet isn't just about the right ingredients, it's about slowing down, stilling your inner to-do list enough so you can listen.

These days, we're talking more than ever—but is anyone listening? The ever-present cell phone provides text messages, video chats, and voice messages, not to mention actual phone calls! The average American spends 1,300 hours on social media a year. And anyone with a computer can make their own radio show through podcasting.

We're made for connection by a Creator who is fundamentally oriented toward connection, both with Himself and with others. And we were made in His relational image!

> *Then God said, "Let us make mankind in our image, in our likeness."*
> GENESIS 1:26 NIV

Speaking and listening is intentionally woven into Creation. As image bearers, one of the ways we communicate not just our own need for connection but also His very image is by speech. And so does He. He created us, immediately blessed us, and spoke to us.

He.

Spoke.

To us.

And we listened.

Wow! Doesn't that blow your mind?

God spoke all of Creation into existence. All Creation not only listened, but also obeyed. God saw that Adam alone was not good (which, so far in the Creation story, is in sharp relief to "And it was good"). So God created Eve as his helper, someone he could talk to. The first thing Adam did when he arose and saw his companion? He spoke!

This is now bone of my bones
and flesh of my flesh;
she shall be called "woman,"
for she was taken out of man.
GENESIS 2:23 NIV

Jesus Christ, the second Adam, the Word made flesh, functioned principally on this same rhythm of speaking and listening. He spoke what He heard God say to Him, nothing more, nothing less.

"For I have not spoken on my own authority, but the Father who sent me
has himself given me a commandment—what to say and what to speak."
JOHN 12:49 ESV

We're still listening, thousands of years later.

I write all of this, dear hearts, because we can be convinced that seeking someone to listen to you is selfish. It can seem like a whiny "What about me?" I confess that, in a fit of self-deprecation, I say to myself, "If I was worth listening to, wouldn't they already be listening?" But let's look at Jesus Himself. Wasn't what He said worth listening to? And yet, look at what He said about that. And bear in mind He was also repeating what God had said, word for word, to the children of Israel generations before Jesus walked.

"For the heart of this people has become dull,
With their ears they scarcely hear,
And they have closed their eyes,
Otherwise they would see with their eyes,
Hear with their ears,
Understand with their heart, and return,
And I would heal them."
MATTHEW 13:15 NASB (SEE ALSO ISAIAH 6:10)

If people didn't listen to God, or Jesus, then they certainly won't always listen to you. While it's good for us to examine whether our speech is worthy of being broadcast, whether it's received or not is not the best barometer of its worthiness.

Here's an important question: Do we listen? We know that communication requires participation from at least two parties. God has been broadcasting to us from the day He knit us together. But are we keeping an ear open to Him? Or are we the only ones talking? God warns us that if that two-way street is blocked in one lane, a full boulevard shutdown is nigh.

"For the eyes of the Lord are on the righteous and his ears are attentive to their prayer, but the face of the Lord is against those who do evil" (I Peter 3:12 NIV; See also Psalm 34:15-16).

Let's say, though, that you're now growing restless. I've done all that! I'm saying true things. I'm obeying the Lord. I've listened to Him. I've listened to others. But I'm not being listened to! I need to be listened to!

Well, here's a question you may not like: do you? Do you need another person to listen to you? Look back at the verse Jesus repeated from the scroll of Isaiah. Even if you're saying the truest of things, some may not be able to hear you. This is a hard truth, my friend, and believe me, I'm speaking to my own heart in addition to yours. But God has promised to listen! His ears are attentive to our prayers. And so perhaps we should change our prayer from "please make them listen to me" to "please open their ears to hear You, Lord." Because to hear God is the beginning of listening to truth altogether.

> ## To hear God is the beginning of listening to truth altogether.

In the meantime, rejoice with me, darling. The eternal ears of heaven are tuned into your frequency. Every cry for help and every song of thanksgiving is music to His ears. This recipe for Lamb Pulao requires you to listen just as I listen to the sizzle of those grains of rice to know just when it's time for the next phase. He's listening with an ear for the very best gift to help you become the very best version of yourself you can be. You are never, ever alone, and thus, you always have Someone willing to listen to you. Even if your phone died, your internet went out, you gave your old school phones to a thrift shop years ago and everyone in your family is out of town . . . If you need to be listened to, He is listening!

Lamb Pulao (Pilaf)

SERVINGS: 8 TO 10 SERVINGS | **TOTAL TIME:** 1 HOUR 45 MINUTES | **ACTIVE TIME:** 1 HOUR

For the lamb

2 pounds lamb shoulder or leg of lamb, cut into 1½ inch pieces

1 large yellow onion, sliced thinly

1 1-inch thumb ginger, chopped finely

6 cloves garlic, sliced thinly

1 serrano chili, sliced in half lengthwise

1 large tomato, chopped

¼ cup coriander seeds

1½ tablespoons fennel seeds

1 teaspoon caraway seeds

6 whole cloves

1 2-inch piece cinnamon

4 cardamom pods, gently crushed

Kosher salt

Chicken stock, as needed

1 chicken bouillon cube (optional)

For the pulao

3 cups basmati rice

¼ cup ghee or avocado oil

4 green cardamom pods, gently crushed

6 whole cloves

1 2-inch piece cinnamon

2 bay leaves

1 large yellow onion, sliced into thin half moons

2 tablespoons ginger garlic paste

2 serrano chilis

½ cup chopped cilantro leaves and soft stems

Toasted cashews, fried onions and plain whole yogurt to garnish

1. Place lamb, onions, ginger, garlic, chili, and tomato in stovetop or electric pressure cooker. Cover with 4 cups of water and 2 teaspoons kosher salt. Place coriander seeds, fennel seeds, caraway seeds, whole cloves, cinnamon, and cardamom pods in a large square of muslin. Tie the ends together to form a little pouch, and toss into the pot too. Cover, lock the lid in place, and make sure valve is set to seal. Pressure cook on high for 30 minutes, then carefully release the pressure by moving the valve to release.

2. Meanwhile, pour rice into a large bowl. Cover with cool water, and gently swirl your hands through the water, rubbing the rice to release extra starch. Strain, then repeat 3 more times until the water runs clear. Cover with water again; soak for 30 minutes on your counter. Strain and allow rice to drain for another 20 minutes.

3. Once pressure cooker is fully released, strain the meat and stock through a colander, reserving the liquid. Remove meat to a bowl and set aside. Squeeze down on remaining vegetable solids

and spice pouch to extract as much flavor as possible. Discard. Measure the liquid; we need 6 cups. Add chicken stock as needed to make up 6 cups of cooking liquid. Dissolve chicken bouillon cube, if using, in the stock. Taste for seasoning, and add salt as you like. Set aside and keep warm.

4. Set a large Dutch oven over medium-high heat. Add ghee or avocado oil and heat until shimmering. Add green cardamom pods, cloves, cinnamon and bay leaves, and cook until fragrant, about 10 seconds. Traditionally we leave the spices in the pot, but if you prefer you can remove them.

5. Add onions and a pinch of salt; cook until translucent and softened, about 4 to 5 minutes.

6. Now add the drained rice. Stir gently to coat each grain in the fragranced fat. Cook until water evaporates from the grains and they don't clump together anymore, about 2 minutes.

7. Stir in the ginger-garlic paste and the serrano chilis, then add the meat. Give the whole pot a good stir and make sure everything is evenly coated in the spices, ginger-garlic paste, and onions.

8. Pour in the stock, along with half the cilantro. Stir well. Bring to a boil, then turn heat down to low so the pot is simmering, cover, cook for 15 minutes until rice is cooked through.

9. Garnish with cilantro, cashews, and fried onions. Best served with a dollop of plain yogurt!

CHAPTER 37

When You Need to Let Go

This devotional cookbook has been written in a handful of coffee shops across Raleigh, North Carolina. As I type, temperatures have dropped. While I'm still in sandals, a cozy sweatshirt keeps my arms warm. The ubiquitous scents of cinnamon, clove, nutmeg, and sugar hang in the air–the telltale evidence of yet another pumpkin spice latte. What a fitting picture of that moment before you let go of summer: toes wiggling free in the last bits of sunshine, heart yearning for the warmth of woodsy spices and thick, frothed milk!

Change is the one thing about our lives that never changes.

What, beloved, are you holding onto?

Why, beloved, are you holding on to it?

Where, beloved, will it go when you let it go?

When, beloved, will you let it go?

Who, beloved, will take care of it once you let it go?

At any given moment, we're in a tug of war between the now and the not yet. It's difficult to know what to hold onto and what to let go, right? For you and me, siblings in the body of the eternal, it's perhaps even harder! Why? Well, if . . .

"every good gift and every perfect gift is from above" (James 1:17 ESV) and

"we know that all things work together for the good of those who love God, who are called according to His purpose" (Romans 8:28 CSB),

then, how do I know what gift to hold onto, and what gift to let go? If everything is from God, should I hold on to . . . everything?

Let's go to the wise guy himself, King Solomon, to figure that out. He didn't lack for gifts from God, right?

> *There is a time for everything, and a season for every activity under the heavens . . . a time to search and a time to give up, a time to keep and a time to throw away.*
> ECCLESIASTES 3:1, 6 NIV

Change is the one thing about our lives that never changes.

Not every gift, not everything God gives us is forever! He that giveth also taketh away-eth. (Anyone else always add the extra "eth"?) He transforms gifts that sit roughly on our palate into delicacies whose sweetness works for our good. And so, let's hold onto everything He gives us with a light grip, knowing that His hands are always moving in our lives. Some things will linger because they still teach. Some things disappear when they no longer serve. Some things will transform to remind us that He who created us out of dust can take even the worst situation and turn it for good.

> *It may be hard for an egg to turn into a bird: it would be a jolly sight harder for a bird to learn to fly while remaining an egg. We are like eggs at present. And you cannot go on indefinitely being just an ordinary, decent egg. We must be hatched or go bad.*
> —C.S. LEWIS

We don't always know what time it is. I have no less than three time-telling devices within my field of vision right now, and I still lose track of time! I follow God's perfect timing even more imperfectly! Solomon recognized that the changing seasons are instructive of more than just our coffee orders or fashion choices. They're emblematic of our own seasonality. Just as the earth thrives through shifting seasons, so do we! The rhythms of tilling the soil, planting the seed, tending the saplings, and harvesting the fruit always leads to letting the winter take the growth you've tended, so you can rest and recuperate. There's a time to hold, and there's a time to let go. If you flipped to this page, then I think you already know what time it is.

Let's hold onto everything He gives us with a light grip, knowing that His hands are always moving in our lives.

You know it's the end of the season. It may hurt. It may be scary. It may even feel wrong. I know this feeling oh too well, sweet friend. But He who gave you this gift will also work your surrender of that gift for your good. It may feel like you're releasing it into the wild unknown, but that's not true: you're releasing it into His hands, and if you are His, then you know His hands almost as well as you know the back of your own! We can do this with confidence because we know Him. We can do this with excitement because we know He has something new for us in the new season. If we let go in obedience to Him, we know God has not only something new for us but something more!

"And everyone who has left houses or brothers or sisters or
father or mother or children or lands, for my name's sake, will
receive a hundredfold and will inherit eternal life."
MATTHEW 19:29 ESV

What you are letting go of, in His Name, makes room for what He has for you next.
So, what, beloved, are you holding on to? You know well. He knows best.
Why, beloved, are you holding on to it? You know well. He knows best.
Where, beloved, will it go when you let it go? You don't know. He knows.
When, beloved, will you let it go? Well, now would be a good time, yes?
Who, beloved, will take care of it once you let it go? He will.

"Remember not the former things, nor consider the things of old.
Behold, I am doing a new thing; now it springs forth, do you not perceive
it? I will make a way in the wilderness and rivers in the desert."
ISAIAH 43:18-19 ESV

YOUR TURN

First ingredients: a pen and a piece of paper. Write down what or who you need to let go. Grab a metal bowl and your piece of paper and take it outside. Sit with it. Thank God for what you've written. Ask Him to show you what good has come. Ask for Him to take it from you.

Last ingredient: something that makes fire. Burn that piece of paper. Feel everything you need to feel. Think everything you need to think. Say everything you need to say.

Now *let go*. Walk away. It is finished.

Are you thirsty, beloved? Let's make something to drink.

The kumquat is a great teacher when it comes to change. These bite-size fruit look like tiny oval oranges and are meant to be eaten whole, peel and all. Your first bite will make you regret it. Extreme bitterness greets you and your lips will pucker! But stay with it. The flavor, you guessed it, changes! The bitterness slowly gives way to happy sweetness, with a side of gratitude that the bitterness is all over. Snack on a couple as you make this spritzer, and consider what you may need to let go of in order to embrace change in your life.

> We know He has something new for us in the new season.

Kumquat & Clove Spritzer

MAKES 4 SERVINGS | TOTAL TIME: 40 MINUTES | ACTIVE TIME: 10 MINUTES

1 cup granulated cane or white sugar

1 cup water

2 teaspoons pink peppercorns

1 teaspoon whole cloves (about 30)

12 kumquats

8 to 10 sprigs of mint

Ice

20 ounces soda water (recommended: Topo Chico)

1. Combine sugar, water, pink peppercorns, and whole cloves in a small saucepan. Set over medium-high heat and bring to a boil. Turn heat down to a simmer, and cook for 5 minutes, uncovered.

2. Remove from heat, and allow the syrup to steep for 30 minutes. Strain, discarding the solids.

3. To build a drink, slice 3 kumquats thinly and drop into an 8-ounce glass. Add 3 tablespoons of syrup. Muddle together, breaking down the kumquats gently. Smack a sprig of mint between your hands to release the fragrant oils. Drop it into the glass along with a few cubes of ice. Stir in 4 to 5 ounces of soda water. Serve!

CHAPTER 38

When You Need a Promise

Cross my heart and hope to die, stick a needle in my eye. *Maa Kasam* (Hindi for "I swear on my mother"). Pinky swear. Hand to God. Shake on it. Sign here. I do so solemnly swear.

Sometimes "I said" is not enough.

Living with so much uncertainty in this world makes us crave a sure thing, a promise, a guarantee. And praise God, not only is He the God of promises, but He also takes it a step further. He is the God of *covenants*. In the ancient world, a covenant was serious business, a binding agreement entered into by two parties, akin to our modern-day air-tight contract. The covenant was marked by ritual, called "The Cut Covenant" (go look it up if you have a strong stomach), a reference to the shedding of actual blood to "seal the deal" and demonstrate in vivid living metaphor the capital seriousness of breaking this promise. The Bible, the written history of the relationship between God and mankind, is split into two testaments, marked by the making of two covenants, the old and the new. Even our historical timeline is counted and divided by His promises: B.C. and A.D.!

> He is the God of covenants.

Promises are an integral way God communes with His children.

Not a single one of all the good promises the LORD had given to the family of Israel was left unfulfilled; everything He had spoken came true.
JOSHUA 21:45 NLT

Here, Joshua refers to the promises of the Mosaic covenant, all of which God kept and delivered. Why is that important? We all know people who talk a big game, make promises, and don't keep them. Not God. Joshua trusts God because of His track record: He showed Himself to be worthy of our trust. And don't miss this part: Joshua and Caleb were the only adult men who got to enter the land God promised the Israelites. Even though Israel had broken their promises, God did not throw His away. He was as He declared He was! He is *the* promise keeper!

"Indeed, I have spoken it; I will also bring it to pass.
I have purposed it; I will also do it."
ISAIAH 46:11 NKJV

I know my own faithlessness. Part of me rues the day that we taught our daughters the biblical concept that our yes should be yes, etc. Should I forget that I'd said they could watch a show after we got home, and I forget, out comes the Bible verse! Ack!

Hey, at least they get it. One of the Ten Commandments is "You shall not lie" because, well, we do! We lie. We forget. We change our minds. And perhaps that's why Jesus cautioned to choose our words wisely. If saying "yes" and really meaning "no" is declared "from the evil one" (Matthew 5:37 NKJV), then imagine the enormous heavenly reverberations of "I promise"! Whether it's as formal as a wedding ceremony or as informal as agreeing to an airport pickup, when we say "I promise," we can feel how it just doubled the weight of our "yes" or "no." The act of speaking these words feels . . . ennobling. And in a way, it is, because it brings us closer to the trustworthy character of God. When He says He promises, He will deliver. And praise God, thanks to the Holy Spirit, our Helper, who leads and guides us in our daily lives, He will empower us to keep our word, even though our default nature may try to wriggle out of it.

> ## Promises are an integral way God communes with His children.

By his divine power, God has given us everything we need for living a godly life. We have received all of this by coming to know Him, the one who called us to Himself by means of His marvelous glory and excellence. And because of His glory and excellence, He has given us great and precious promises. These are the promises that enable you to share His divine nature and escape the world's corruption caused by human desires.
II PETER 1:3-4 NLT

Fundamentally, the Bible is not only a love story, but also one of a promise made and kept. When the first humans broke their promise to God, He promised that He would eventually triumph over the evil that had temporarily driven a schism between humanity and Himself. This is the story of a promise made by the One to whom a promise was not kept . . . a promise made to the promise breakers by the Promise Keeper so that the two would be reconciled and promised to each other forever. If you're in need of a promise, remember that Jesus made a way for you to be forgiven of your wrongdoings, and to have an internal renewal of your heart, and an intimate relationship and knowledge of God. Jesus is the guarantor of this promise, which He paid for with His blood. Someone cares about you so much that not only did He make this new covenant with you when He died on the cross, but He also promised faithfulness even if you stray. This is the biggest, most profound, most expensive promise ever made in history, and it was made to you, for you, and about you! In Christ, we have the promise to end all promises, the surety unending, the only promise we will ever truly need. The cross upon our heart. Forevermore. Amen.

When He says He promises, He will deliver.

Birria is a Mexican braised meat dish (usually goat) that often is served at wedding feasts—a celebration made between two people and witnessed by the guests. As you prepare this dish, consider the promise made, sealed, and guaranteed by Jesus for you. How does that make you feel? What does that tell you about where you are right now?

Beef Birria-style Tacos

SERVINGS: 18 TACOS | **TOTAL TIME:** 3 HOURS | **ACTIVE TIME:** 1 HOUR 30 MINUTES

3 pounds boneless beef chuck roast, trimmed of excess fat, cut into 2-inch chunks

Kosher salt

10 dried California or New Mexico chilis

2 dried guajillo chilis

2 dried ancho chilis

2 black cardamom pods (optional)

1 large white onion, sliced in half

6 cloves garlic, chopped

1 2-inch piece fresh ginger, chopped

¼ cup apple cider vinegar

1 tablespoon toasted sesame seeds

1 tablespoon garam masala

½ teaspoon black peppercorns

1 teaspoon dried Mexican oregano

1 teaspoon toasted cumin seeds

¼ cup avocado oil

4 cups beef broth

18 corn tortillas

Large handful of cilantro including soft stems, minced

2 limes, sliced into wedges

1 pound Chihuahua, Oaxaca, or Monterey jack cheese, shredded

1. Season beef chunks well with salt and pepper. Set aside. Stem and seed the dried chilis.

2. Place the chilis, black cardamom pods, half the white onion, garlic, and ginger in a medium saucepan. Cover with 6 cups of water, then bring to a boil. Turn down to a vigorous simmer and cook, uncovered, for 10 minutes, pushing the chilis down every now and then.

3. Meanwhile, set electric pressure cooker to sauté on HIGH (or stovetop pressure over a high flame). Add 2 tablespoons oil, and when just starting to smoke, add half of the beef, making sure not to crowd the pot. Cook until nicely browned on a few sides, about 10 minutes. Remove to a plate and repeat with remaining beef.

4. Using a slotted spoon, add chilis and remaining solids to a blender along with 2 cups of cooking liquid, apple cider vinegar, sesame seeds, peppercorns, oregano, cumin seeds, and garam masala. Cover and blend until smooth. Strain the sauce over a bowl, pressing down on the solids to extract as much sauce as possible. Discard the solids.

5. Add all the beef back to the pressure cooker, along with chili-spice paste, beef broth, and 2 teaspoons of kosher salt. Lock the lid in place, make sure vent is set to SEAL, and cook on high pressure for 40 minutes. Once done, allow to naturally release for 15 minutes before carefully quick releasing remaining pressure.

6. Finely chop remaining onion. Shred the beef and adjust for seasoning.

7. To make tacos: heat a nonstick frying pan over medium heat. Dip both sides of a tortilla into the beef broth. Sprinkle cheese evenly across one side, top with some shredded beef, then drizzle with a little more broth. Place on the frying pan, and once the cheese has melted, fold the tortilla in half. Cook on both sides until browned and crispy. Garnish with finely chopped onion, cilantro, and a squeeze of lime. Serve with bowls of the broth to dip some more!

CHAPTER 39

When You Need Power

A few years ago, I witnessed a miracle. A woman who had never attended our church came to our women's retreat. She was a young woman, a mother of three, who had suddenly been debilitated by a mystery illness and confined to a wheelchair. Test after test revealed no answers. One night she had a dream that she was dancing in a field of tulips. A few days later she saw that our retreat was in a hotel next to an enormous tulip field. That night, a few women committed to praying for her without ceasing. The next morning, as we gathered for the morning teaching, suddenly the foot-thumping baseline of "Shout" by the Isley Brothers came over the speakers . . . and that very woman started dancing down the aisle and onto the stage! She was healed (and remains so to this day)! I still can't believe it. But I will never forget that awesome demonstration of God's power.

> Jesus had power that caused wonder, consternation, joy, and anger.

Jesus had power that caused wonder, consternation, joy, and anger. His entire earthly ministry was marked by manifestations of the power of God. There was power in the truth of the things He said, but man, there's something about the miracles that really breaks through the hard heart of disbelief, right? He defied the laws of physics, of reality as we know it. Miracle after miracle seemed to communicate that while we may feel powerless, here was One whose power not only dwarfed our own, but confounded even what we thought power was capable of!

> *"Do not believe me unless I do the works of my Father. But if I do them, even though you do not believe me, believe the works, that you may know and understand that the Father is in me, and I in the Father."*
> JOHN 10:37–38 NIV

Jesus' miracles weren't necessarily simply to release the oppressed from suffering, but to testify to the very nature of God. They worked like Creation, which reveals:

God's invisible qualities—His eternal power and divine nature—
have been clearly seen, being understood from what has
been made, so that people are without excuse.
ROMANS 1:20 NIV

Consider this moment in the Gospel of Luke. Jesus is walking through a throng of people, with His disciples alongside Him, and then He asks, "Who touched Me?" Peter says, very reasonably, that there are people all around him (they're in a crowd, after all).

But Jesus said, "Someone touched Me; I know that power has gone out from Me."
LUKE 8:46 NIV

Jesus doing the impossible over and over again is one thing. When He made the blind to see and the lame to walk, He exerted His power with intention and focus, moving in and by God's direction. Here, though, a woman who never stopped bleeding touched Him . . . and stopped bleeding! She was healed even though He wasn't paying attention to her. And so to me, this indicates that Jesus didn't merely have power. He was power. He was a powerhouse!

> Jesus didn't merely have power. He was power. He was a powerhouse!

If we need power, we need Jesus. God is well aware of your lack of power, your need you came right here to this page to find. God has what you need, is what you need. It's even in His name! One of the principal names for God is El, which means "The" in Hebrew and is rooted in the word for power. One of the names of God, El Shaddai, doubles down on this: The Powerful One Who Gives Power. God nurtures us with His power through intimacy with Him. And if we look at the intimate relationship Jesus had with the Father, I think we can see one of the key ways we can access that power too. God is power and feeds His people power from His own power.

If you're not feeling powerful right now, remember that if you have daily surrendered your life to Him, He has already exerted His power to free you from the power of sin in your life. That's already done, and yet there is so much more available to you, oh weary one.

He gives power to the faint, and to him who has no might he increases strength.
ISAIAH 40:29 ESV

The greatest work of power in human history is working on and within you.
Take that in for a second.

Jesus' power was greater than any patriarch, any prophet that came before Him, so great all of human history now is separated into two parts based on His earthly life. And perhaps the great work of that greatest power ever known was His resurrection, because not only did it defy the one certainty of all our lives (death), but it also eliminated the power of sin to keep us separated from Him forever. He ascended into heaven and is seated at the right hand of the Father, El Shaddai Himself. And because God is always thinking about you and me, He didn't just come to earth to display His power, He didn't just die and resurrect in order to break the powers of darkness, but He shares that very same power with you today. Shout, indeed! We've got the power!

> ## He shares that very same power with you today.

Ribeyes with King and Queen Butter

MAKES 2 TO 4 SERVINGS | **TOTAL TIME**: 30 TO 50 MINUTES | **ACTIVE TIME**: 30 TO 50 MINUTES

Cook's Note: Did you know that black peppercorns are called the king of spices? And cardamom the queen? This compound butter is fit for royalty, which in days of yore would have been the most powerful people in the land! This technique for cooking steaks is called reverse searing, and it ensures even, coast-to-coast pink every time. Worth the extra time!

Kosher salt and freshly ground black pepper

1 stick (½ cup or 8 tablespoons) unsalted butter, at room temperature

2 garlic cloves, grated on a microplane

¾ teaspoon ground green cardamom

¾ teaspoon coarsely ground black pepper

Small handful, 4 to 5 sprigs, cilantro, minced

2 to 4 ribeye steaks, at least 1½ inch thick each

2 tablespoons avocado oil

1. Preheat oven to 250 degrees Fahrenheit.

2. Place butter in a small bowl. Stir in garlic, cardamom, black pepper, cilantro, and a little salt to taste. Taste for seasoning. Cut a rectangle of parchment paper. Place butter at the bottom end of it, then roll tightly. Twist the ends like a piece of candy and freeze.

3. Pat the steaks dry with paper towels and sprinkle both sides and edges of the steaks generously with salt and pepper. Line a sheet pan with foil or parchment paper, and set a flat wire rack in it. Lay steaks on the wire rack and pop into the oven. Cook until the center of the steaks registers 105 degrees Fahrenheit (rare), 115 degrees Fahrenheit (medium-rare), 125 degrees Fahrenheit (medium), or 135 degrees Fahrenheit (medium well). This can take anywhere from 25 to 45 minutes.

4. When steaks reach desired temperature remove from the oven. Set a large cast iron skillet over medium-high to high heat. Add avocado oil and heat until just beginning to smoke. Add the steaks and cook until each side is beautifully brown, 1 to 1½ minutes a side. Don't forget the edges! Sear those too. Serve right away with slices of King and Queen butter on top.

CHAPTER 40

When You Need Mercy

You pity the fool because you don't want to beat up a fool! You know, pity is between sorry and mercy. See, if you pity him, you know, you won't have to beat him up. So that's why I say fools, you gotta give another chance because they don't know no better. That's why I pity them!

—MR. T

There are many times that I thank God that He isn't like us. Reading this quote from Mr. T is just one of them! There's an experience peculiar to Jesus-people that I honestly didn't have until He took hold of my heart—being thoroughly and entirely sick of myself. Have you ever experienced that, friend? It's a specific moment where you realize that no matter how hard you try, you just can't do any better, and in fact, when you do, you just make things worse. You kinda reach the end of yourself, and the end isn't pretty. Our ancestors may have called it grieving over our sin. Whatever you call it, in those moments, I've learned to reach out to God for a touch of His mercy, a little reassurance that He's still for me even though I've fallen so short of the mark. First, the good news. God is merciful to all.

> *The LORD is good to all, and his mercy is over all that he has made.*
> PSALM 145:9 ESV

But, and this is both good and bad news, depending on who you are, there are tiers to His mercy plan. Let's scan further down in this same psalm of David:

> *The LORD is near to all who call on him,*
> *to all who call on him in truth.*
> *He fulfills the desire of those who fear him;*
> *he also hears their cry and saves them.*
> *The LORD preserves all who love him,*
> *but all the wicked he will destroy.*
> PSALM 145:18-20 ESV

God's mercy is different for different types of people. There's a general mercy, a common grace, where God holds back evil from running this place with all His might, and for that we can give thanks because as hard as life is now, imagine if He pulled His hand away?

But there's also a special mercy reserved for those who "call on Him in truth," "fear Him," and "love Him." For those in honest, wise, right relationship with Him, God gifts kinship, proximity, responsiveness, and protection. For those defined by the opposite of that posture, God withholds this mercy. My heart quivers at this truth, because I don't like to exclude anyone, but we cannot appreciate what we have unless we consider what it would be like not to have it. God is, and always has been, very particular about His mercy. As He said through Moses and through Paul:

> "I will have mercy on whom I have mercy, and I will have
> compassion on whom I have compassion."
> ROMANS 9:15 ESV (SEE ALSO EXODUS 33:19.)

As a lover of doing, and to-do lists, I can feel my fingers itching to create a to-do list to put me in that first category of people. I know what I want, how do I get it? More good and bad news, darlings. We are do-ers by nature: foragers, hunters, gatherers, sleuths, prospectors! And yet, Paul cautions us against it:

> "So then it depends not on human will or exertion, but on God, who has mercy."
> ROMANS 9:16 ESV

God's mercy is not earned but given.

We need mercy. We all do. And the good news is we all get some version of it.

God's mercy is not earned but given.

God still "makes his sun rise on the evil and on the good, and sends rain on the just and on the unjust" (Matthew 5:45 ESV). Jesus said this while exhorting His followers to love their enemies, in imitation of their heavenly Father. So as ones in right relationship with God, as ones learning to mimic His goodness, we too must bestow this common mercy to all. If, as David pointed out, we are in honest, wise, and right relationship with our Father, then we must show mercy even to those who don't seem to deserve it.

> For judgment is without mercy to one who has shown
> no mercy. Mercy triumphs over judgment.
> JAMES 2:13 ESV

If we need mercy, we must show it. And ironically, in some cases, when someone has hurt us deeply, we might need God's mercy in order to show mercy! We could never equal God's capacity, but He does ask us to pour out the love and mercy we have taken from Him and make it part of the daily bread we share! And because His mercy is infinite, the good news is that He lavishes us with as much as we need, both for ourselves and to bestow upon others.

If I withhold mercy, I have lost touch with the gospel. I have lost touch with God's undeserved kindness and pardon.

JOHN STOTT

Close your eyes and ask God to give you a vision for the mercy He has given you. What does it look like? How does He show you mercy?

Now, ask Him to whom He wants you to show mercy. How does that feel? Do you need His help to do so? Keep all of these thoughts in mind and reflect on them as you make this delicious coriander-orange tea cake.

One of God's most memorable acts of mercy was to the Israelites in the desert, when He supplied them with food in the form of *manna*. Scholars today think that it was some form of coriander, that warm, lemon-and-grass flavored spice. It's most often used in savory cooking, but I think it's a lovely counterpoint in desserts, like this coriander-orange tea cake. As you grind the seeds to a fine powder, take in their warm aromas. Can you imagine the Israelites smelling the coriander as they gathered God's mercy every day?

> His mercy is infinite, and the good news is that He lavishes us with as much as we need.

Coriander-Orange Tea Cake

MAKES 8 SERVINGS | **TOTAL TIME:** 2 HOURS 15 MINUTES | **ACTIVE TIME:** 1 HOUR 15 MINUTES

Cook's Note: You can make this with any orange you like, as long as you use 600g of them. This comes to about 2 navel oranges.

600g/1.3 pounds oranges (see Cook's Note)

2 tablespoons coriander seeds, ground to a medium-fine powder

1 ¼ teaspoon baking powder

6 large eggs, at room temperature

250g (1 ¼ cups) granulated cane or white sugar

250g (2 ¾ cups) almond flour

Creme fraiche to serve

1. Preheat oven to 325 degrees Fahrenheit. Grease and line a 9-inch cake pan with parchment paper.

2. Place oranges in a large saucepan and cover with cool water. Bring to a boil over medium-high heat, and boil for 40 minutes, ensuring that the oranges are moving and cooking evenly throughout, adding more hot water when level goes below the oranges themselves. Strain the oranges through a colander, and then rinse. Allow to cool. Roughly chop the cooked oranges, removing all the seeds. Allow to cool completely.

3. Drop chopped oranges into a food processor, and pulse, scraping down the sides periodically, until pureed to a marmalade-like consistency.

4. Add ground coriander, baking powder, eggs, sugar, and almond flour, and process for 20 seconds until well combined.

5. Pour the cake batter into the lined cake pan. Bake in the center of the oven for 60 minutes, or until the surface is golden and a toothpick inserted into the center comes out clean.

6. Place cake pan on a wire rack to cool completely. Be careful when you turn out the cake, because the surface will be sticky! Slice and serve with a dollop of creme fraiche and a cup of tea.

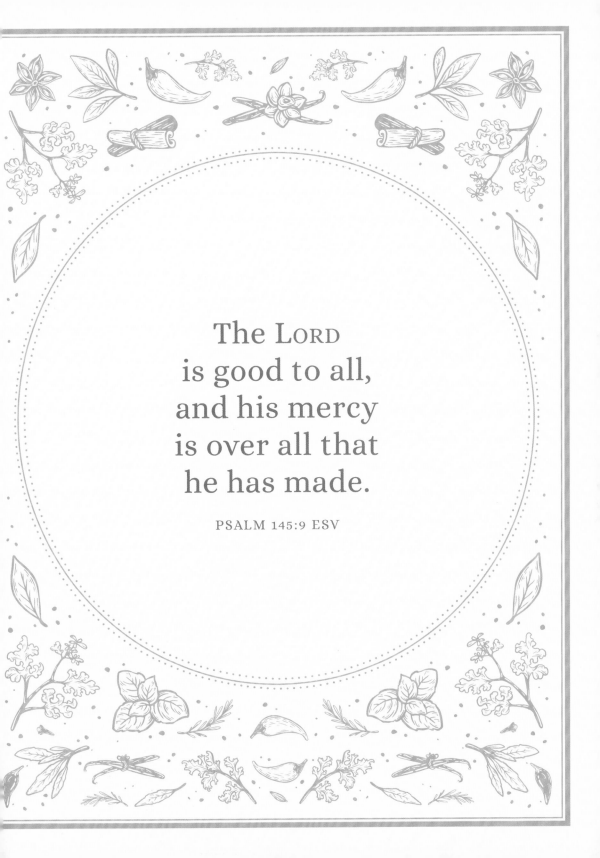

The LORD
is good to all,
and his mercy
is over all that
he has made.

PSALM 145:9 ESV

When You Need to Celebrate

CHAPTER 41

When You Need to Celebrate

I grew up thinking of God as, well, a party pooper.

Informed by Renaissance-era paintings and Hollywood movies alike, to me, God was a very serious, somber, grumpy celestial being. Lips always turned downward, brow forming an eleven at the bridge of the nose, easily irritated . . . This was not One who was into celebrations because there was just so much evil in the world, how could He? There's no time to celebrate! We've got work to do! To put it in comic book hero terms (come on, I know some of you love them as much as I do!), God was more Batman than Thor.

This image was further reinforced by a scarring incident in my childhood. Freshly promoted in the Catholic tradition to start lining up for communion with the rest of the body, I did the unthinkable: I dropped it. The deacon, a very pious Italian man, looked at me as if I had kicked Jesus Himself in the stomach. From then on, I never went to take communion from him, even if it meant walking all the way around to another line on the other side of the sanctuary. Oh the irony! The only celebration I'd heard of when it came to God was to "celebrate" the sacrament of the Eucharist . . . and here I'd gone and been the party pooper myself!

That grim-faced Batman of a God couldn't be further from the truth. Our God likes to party. So let's get this party started, shall we?

The Hebrew word for celebrate is *hagag*, and it implies not just a party but giddiness! God commanded His people to such feasts of giddiness multiple times a year, and each one was intricately connected to Himself—they were feasts of thanksgiving and remembrance.

They sang His praises! They danced! They celebrated!

The first use of the word in Scripture is deeply significant of just how seriously God takes celebrations. Moses and Aaron approach Pharaoh for the first time, requesting he let the Israelites go celebrate a feast to God in the wilderness.

*Afterward Moses and Aaron went and said to Pharaoh, "Thus
says the Lord, the God of Israel, 'Let my people go, that they may
hold a feast to me in the wilderness.' But Pharaoh said, "Who is
the LORD, that I should obey his voice and let Israel go?"*

EXODUS 5:1-2 ESV

This was the beginning of the epic confrontation between Pharaoh and God's proxy, Moses . . . over a celebration! Seven plagues and an angel of death later, God launched a dramatic escape plan for His children that included the cinematic parting of the Red Sea. And guess what the Israelites did as soon as they were free? They sang His praises! They danced! They celebrated!

*"Then Miriam the prophetess, Aaron's sister, took a timbrel [aka a tamborine]
in her hand, and all the women followed her, with timbrels and dancing."*

EXODUS 15:20 NIV

After that, God commands them to celebrate Passover (Exodus 12:14), to remember! Celebrations remind us of God's goodness! God wants us to remember Him in His wholeness. Yes, He is firm about the Law and sin. But He is also a good, kind, and joyful God, and He wants us to remember that, to always connect joy with the Joy-giver!

If God likes to party, then our identity, as His children, is that of party people! Passover is the biggest event on the Jewish calendar. How meaningful that a foundational element of the Jewish identity—the people that God rescued—is marked by a feast! God asked them to celebrate every year, not just so they wouldn't forget where they came from so to speak, but so they would remember Him with joy and thanksgiving! Not with guilt and shame! Or retribution and punishment! But with joy in their hearts and a song on their lips. The story is retold at the Passover table by reading the Haggadah—do you see the same root word, *hagag,* to celebrate with giddiness? As followers and lovers of Jesus, we are also marked by Passover. Jesus' Last Supper was a Passover celebration. How significant that His last meal with His disciples, the one where He tried to explain the spiritual significance of what was about to happen (His death), was not any run-of-the-mill dinner, but a *feast!*

Celebrating, even when it's not an overtly spiritual celebration, should be aimed at God, because every good and perfect gift is from above! A promotion, a health prognosis, a birthday, an anniversary. Here's the hard part though: even when something difficult has happened, we need to view that as a good and perfect gift from above

> Celebrations
> remind us of
> God's goodness!

because the story isn't over. As Joseph so pithily put it, what appears to be for our harm, God works for our good. Yes, it's hard to do. It might not even seem appropriate. If you have the strength to do it though, it will help you through it, because it keeps your eyes on the long term instead of the short term. And perhaps that's the purpose of all the celebrating during the good times; it ingrains in our marrow that our God is good, trustworthy, one who gives good gifts. We can draw on that marrow when our bones are weak.

One of the ways we can distinguish ourselves as people who follow God is to be in a constant state of gratitude to Him. We give credit where it's due, so we don't take credit for it or give it to an idol. Being thankful keeps us in the state of being joyful, and being joyful makes us wanna celebrate. When we don't, we run the risk of our minds and hearts darkening and turning away from Him.

Even though they knew God, they did not honor Him as God or give thanks, but they became futile in their reasonings, and their senseless hearts were darkened.

ROMANS 1:21 NASB

And so, if you're in the mood to celebrate, in the eternal words of Wayne's World, party on dude! You are cleared for take-off. Just remember to turn your hoots and hollers heaven-ward to the Source of Celebration. But, dearest heart, if you're not in the mood to celebrate, if you long to be in a celebratory state of mind, consider the story of the Prodigal Son. The father, overjoyed that his son had returned, ran toward him while he was still a long way off, commanding the slaughter of the fattened calf, the one they'd been saving for months for a special occasion. To our Father, you are worthy of that kind of celebration! Isn't that magnificent?! Right now, He's running toward you with the finest robe, the ring of authority, the choicest meat. A lavish celebration happened in heaven when Jesus grabbed your heart, and an even more elaborate one awaits all of us when we feast with Him in eternity. Even if your heart is too heavy to rejoice, know that He rejoices over you. That's a reason to celebrate.

> God is good, kind, and joyful, and we should always connect joy with the Joy-giver!

The LORD your God is in your midst,
a mighty one who will save;
he will rejoice over you with gladness;
he will quiet you by his love;
he will exult over you with loud singing.

ZEPHANIAH 3:17 ESV

UNWIND

Growing up, whenever lamb was on the dinner table, I knew we were celebrating! It's an integral part of the Passover meal too. I know lamb can seem intimidating. This recipe is very easy but still feels like a celebration, which is my favorite kind of dish. The bittersweet salad is a nod to the traditional bitter herbs and sweet fruit and nut paste that are part of a traditional Passover feast.

Lamb Shawarma-ish
with Bittersweet Salad

ACTIVE TIME: 50 TO 60 MINUTES | **TOTAL TIME:** 2 HOURS 45 MINUTES

Kosher salt

2 teaspoons cumin seeds

¾ teaspoon black
peppercorns

3 whole cloves

6 green cardamom pods

¾ teaspoon fennel seeds

½ cinnamon stick

2 teaspoons sweet paprika

2 teaspoons grated ginger
(from a 1½-inch thumb of
ginger)

1½ teaspoons grated garlic
(from about 3 medium cloves
garlic)

3 tablespoons lemon juice
(about ½ a lemon's worth)

5 tablespoons extra virgin
olive oil

1 3 to 4-pound butterflied,
boneless leg of lamb

Bittersweet salad

2 hearts of romaine lettuce,
tough outer leaves removed,
ripped into 1-inch pieces

1 small head radicchio, core
removed, sliced into ½-inch
pieces

1½ cups arugula

Leaves from 6 sprigs mint

No-Fail Vinaigrette (p. xx)

Tahini sauce (see below)

Pita bread for serving

1. Toast cumin, peppercorns, cloves, cardamom pods, fennel seeds, and cinnamon stick in a small frying pan set over medium low heat. Shake the pan and stir, toasting the spices until fragrant, 2 to 3 minutes. Pour onto a plate to cool, then grind to a fine powder in a spice grinder. Pour into a small bowl, and stir in paprika, ginger, garlic, lemon juice, and olive oil, plus 1½ tablespoons kosher salt. Set aside.

2. Place the leg of lamb on your cutting board with the fat cap facing down. Now, using a sharp knife, trim any pockets of fat, connective tissue, and silver skin. Flip the lamb over. Trim fat to a ¼-inch thickness. Pound the meat to an even 1-inch thickness. Finally, slice into the fat cap at ½-inch intervals in a crosshatch patten; cut through the fat but not into the meat.

3. Rub the marinade all over the meat on both sides, being sure to get it between the crosshatches. Line a sheet pan with foil, and place a wire rack in it. Lay the lamb on the rack, fat side up, and allow to sit, uncovered, at room temperature for 45 minutes.

4. Set up your oven: Place one oven rack in the middle of the oven, and another about 6 inches from the broiler element. Preheat to 250 degrees Fahrenheit.

5. When the oven reaches temperature, pop the lamb into the oven. Bake for 45 to 55 minutes, until an instant-read thermometer inserted in the center registers 120 to 125 degrees Fahrenheit. Remove from the oven.

6. Turn the broiler on, and allow the oven to heat up for 10 minutes. Return lamb to the oven on the higher rack, and cook for another 5 minutes until fat is browned and crispy, and lamb registers 125 to 130 degrees Fahrenheit for medium.

7. Pull lamb from the oven, and transfer to carving board (two sets of tongs comes in handy here!). Tent loosely with foil and allow to rest 20 minutes.

8. Meanwhile, make the dressing: combine shallots, rice wine vinegar, and lemon juice with a big pinch of salt in a medium bowl. Allow to sit for 5 minutes. Whisk in dijon mustard and honey, then slowly drizzle in olive oil while whisking continuously. Season well with salt and pepper. Dip a piece of lettuce in the dressing and taste it. Adjust seasoning according to your palate.

9. To build the salad, toss romaine, radicchio, arugula, and whole mint leaves together in a large bowl. Season with salt and pepper. Now add a little dressing at a time, tossing as you go, until the salad is dressed to your liking.

10. Slice lamb vertically into 3 equal pieces. Then slice each of those against the grain. Serve on a large platter with pita bread and tahini sauce, alongside big bowl of salad.

Simple tahini sauce

¼ cup tahini

2 tablespoons lemon juice (from 1 to 2 lemons)

¼ cup hot water, plus more as needed

2 tablespoons olive oil

In a medium bowl, whisk together tahini, lemon juice, olive oil together. It will seize up but don't worry! Whisk in hot water, a little at a time, until sauce is luxuriously creamy.

CHAPTER 42

When You Need Thankfulness

M y very first Thanksgiving in the States happened during my freshman year of college. In some ways it felt like any other feast: family gathered around the table, platters of food, and good cheer. But my eyes widened at the larger-than-life nature of the feast itself. A gigantic bird sat in the middle of the table, so much smaller than the roast chicken my mum would serve for Christmas lunch. Multiple bowls of starch: mashed potatoes, stuffing, and then, oh my gosh, is that marshmallows on top of sweet potatoes? It's as close to feeling like an alien as I've ever felt! And yet I marveled that I'd been led to a country that, as hard as it worked, stopped everything for a day to give thanks to God. And when I read Abraham Lincoln's "Thanksgiving Proclamation," I marveled further still at a nation that, in the midst of a war that literally nearly tore itself apart, stopped to give thanks to God.

> Even when all is lost, God's hands are still on my lungs, pulling them open to expand and take in air.

But it's hard to be thankful sometimes, right? Over the past decade the message about thanksgiving unlocking peace and joy has become so widespread that at this point, it can sound trite. Frankly, I've been struggling for the past hour to figure out a fresh, new take on thanksgiving, as much to encourage my heart as to encourage yours. Because, while I may be known for being a bright, sunny person, if you pulled my husband aside at a dinner party and asked him, "Hey what is she really like?" he'd tell you that while my joy is genuine when you see it, I'm pretty prone to seeing the glass half empty.

Why is thankfulness so dang important? First of all, because it keeps our pride in check. But forcing us to take our eyes off ourselves, and onto the One who's really in control, we think of ourselves less often. Pride gets in the way of thanksgiving, but thanksgiving neutralizes pride.

Pride slays Thanksgiving, but a humble mind is the soil out of which thanks naturally grow. A proud man is seldom a grateful man, for he never thinks he gets as much as he deserves.

HENRY WARD BEECHER

When we give thanks, we have to take a long, hard look at everything in our lives, even the things we take for granted. We consider what it would be like to live without eyes, ears, taste buds, hands, feet, a beating heart, breath! Even when all is lost, God's hands are still on my lungs, pulling them open to expand and take in air, squeezing them to expel that which doesn't serve me. When I start to count, I start to realize that while I once only saw scarcity, I actually have riches! My joy increases a little. Maybe the glass isn't half empty.

> Thankfulness keeps us soft, tender, and receptive.

When I first started writing and publishing recipes for Food Network, I'd skim the comments below to see what people thought of it. No matter how many positive reviews the recipe garnered, if there was one negative one, I'd stew over it for days. Perhaps that's why the saying goes, "one rotten apple spoils the whole barrel." Perfectly good apples are tainted! Listen, I'm not suggesting we embody the Church Lady and say, "Isn't that special?" about every hard thing in our lives! There's plenty of room in the Bible for weeping and lamenting. But we can't let those things infect all the good that He has given us, right? We need to keep these things separate in our mind, or actually, maybe allow His goodness to "infect" the hardships in our lives! Thankfulness keeps our hearts in His presence, which keeps them from hardening and turning cynical. It keeps us soft, tender, and receptive. Ingratitude makes us blind to the movements of His hands, deaf to His gentle voice, unwilling to move when He directs us. Eventually, it makes us forget God altogether, and we lose that characteristic that sets us apart, that consecrates us, as followers of The Way: that we are a grateful people, thanking God at all times (Romans 1:18-21). The road of the ungrateful can lead to idolatry because we have forgotten God.

> *They know God, but they do not give Him the honor that belongs to Him, nor do they thank Him. Instead, their thoughts have become complete nonsense, and their empty minds are filled with darkness.*

ROMANS 1:21 GNT

Some of you reading this right now may have broken hearts. How do we adopt a spirit of thankfulness when we are so downtrodden? Let's look at Psalm 28, written by David, who sounds like he's in anguish.

"To You, O Lord, I call; my rock, do not be deaf to me, For if You are silent to me, I will become like those who go down to the pit." (v. 1 NASB)

By the end of the psalm, though, David's spirit has made a dramatic turnaround: "Therefore my heart exults, And with my song I shall thank Him." (v. 7 NASB)

Whoa! What happened in between?

After a prolonged period of David essentially asking God to smite his enemies (have you ever asked God to go take care of a situation the way you thought would be best?), David experienced the backward-and-forward-time-machine that thankfulness offers. By casting our minds back on God's past faithfulness, we're able to look the future in the eye with confidence and gratitude, because God is the same yesterday, today, and forever. His character is never changing, and so, if you're in Christ, then you know He has already come to your rescue at least once in your life. And if He has done it before, He'll do it again.

Thanksgiving does not dismiss the very real difficulties of the moment, all of its trials and pains. But it also acknowledges that the pain is not the whole picture. We start to see what seemed small, what seemed mundane, as epiphanies about His nature. We realize that we bear witness to miracles happening all around us. And so, we aren't giving thanks for the situation necessarily, but for the character of God who walks with us through the situation. Let's face it, sometimes the hardships of our lives can feel so intense that we're doubled over, as if the suffering is draining our very life force. Thanksgiving is life-giving. It refills our cup and strengthens our spine with the truth that God is bigger than our circumstances.

We've seen that David experienced the importance of thanksgiving to his own psyche, but he also knew it was important to the entire nation of Israel, so much so that he commanded Levite priests to make thanksgiving sacrifices at the temple 24/7! In the midst of our trials, thanksgiving can feel like a sacrifice. Praise costs us something. The Hebrew word for praise, *yada*, paints a picture of hands reaching out to heaven. While it may hurt to do that sometimes, when we give thanks and praise, God's hands are reaching right back to us too. He will meet our hands. And that's how our spine straightens, and our life force renews, because we're touching the divine. As followers of Jesus we can say things that no one

> Thanksgiving is life-giving. It refills our cup and strengthens our spine with the truth that God is bigger than our circumstances.

> ## He is working in and through us for His purposes and for our good.

else can: He is with us. He is for us. He lives within us. He is working in and through us for His purposes and for our good.

> *Let them thank the L*ORD *for his steadfast love, for his wondrous works to the children of man! For he satisfies the longing soul, and the hungry soul he fills with good things.*
> PSALM 107:8-9 ESV

Minimalist's Sweet Potato "Casserole"

MAKES 4 SERVINGS | **TOTAL TIME:** 1 HOUR 45 MINUTES | **ACTIVE TIME:** 15 MINUTES

4 medium sweet potatoes or yams, all about the same size

Avocado oil

Ajwain (carom) or cumin seeds

Kosher salt and freshly ground pepper

Garam masala

Mini marshmallows

1. Preheat oven to 300 degrees Fahrenheit.

2. Wash and scrub sweet potatoes. Dry well, and then prick the surface of each yam about 4 to 5 times at somewhat equal intervals. Place on a parchment-lined sheet pan.

3. Drizzle each sweet potato with a glug of oil, a pinch of ajwain or cumin seeds, a good pinch of salt, and a few grinds of black pepper. Massage this mixture all over the tubers, then pop into the oven and roast for about 1½ hours, until caramelized on the bottom and very tender. Remove from the oven, and turn your oven to the broiler setting. Adjust oven rack about 7 inches from the element.

4. Meanwhile, slice sweet potatoes in half, lengthwise, keeping them attached (i.e., don't slice all the way through the skin). Drizzle with a touch more oil, and sprinkle with a little garam masala and salt. Now sprinkle with as many mini marshmallows as you like, and pop back under the broiler, keeping a careful eye on them so they brown but don't combust! Remove from the oven, cool slightly, and then enjoy!

CHAPTER 43

When You Need Something to Give

Maybe people-pleasing isn't the vile character flaw you think it is," my therapist said to me, after I'd confessed how much I hated that part of myself. I'd likened myself to water, instinctually filling the shape of whatever container I happened to find myself in. "Can you see how it's helped you get to this point in your life?"

I paused. Never before had I considered there could be an upside to a character trait I'd only seen vilified as a mark of the weak.

On the one hand, being a people-pleaser has positioned me to speak into my friends' and colleagues' lives at their darkest hour. I've prayed with people who long ago rejected God. I've introduced people to a real-life Christian, rather than the ones they've seen in movies. They've witnessed me walking through titanic times, either clinging to the Lord or openly wrestling with Him.

> Scripture says that our faith is a gift from God, not a skill of our own mustering.

On the other hand, I feel the handcuffs. I am so enslaved to their appreciation of me that I have muzzled myself. For someone who prizes authenticity, I know I've withheld some of the most important aspects of myself from them, for fear that they wouldn't understand and they'd reject me. I'll bend over backward, giving and giving and giving, but also keep a foot hovering over the brakes in case I sense rejection brewing.

Do you relate to being a people pleaser? Do you struggle with this symbiotic parasite that simultaneously fills your dance card, metaphorically speaking, but also leaves you at the mercy of other people's opinions of you?

How do we harness the power of giving ourselves to others without becoming enslaved by it? Let's look at a man who may have felt the tension between pleasing people and pleasing God: the apostle Paul.

I try to please everyone in everything I do...
I CORINTHIANS 10:33 ESV

Paul took advantage of the multiplicity of identities at work within him. He was different things to different people–to the Jew a Jew, to the Greek a Greek. Especially in this day and age, where the divide between people feels impossible to cross, identifying similarities can build a bridge across the crevasse. I mean, that's why I love food so much, not just because it tickles the tastebuds, but because it also knits hearts together no matter what division the minds might feel.

But Paul put limits on pleasing people. Let's read the remainder of that verse:

I try to please everyone in everything I do,
not seeking my own advantage, but that
of many, that they may be saved.
I CORINTHIANS 10:33 ESV

Paul didn't seek to attract hearts to draw people to himself, but to draw them to Christ! He gave of himself so that others would have the chance to receive (or I suppose, reject) the best friend we'll ever have. When I give to others, it's often out of a fear of loneliness or rejection. But in a way, Paul was reaching out and risking being rejected, because his outreach was all about Christ.

If our giving is predicated in any way on reciprocity or a high opinion of ourselves, then we will burn out on giving.

Striving to please Jesus is actually easier, in some ways, than trying to please those around us!

And without faith it is impossible to please him, for whoever would draw near to God must believe that he exists and that he rewards those who seek him.
HEBREWS 11:6 ESV

He is unchanging. His standards don't shift.

This verse always makes me breathe a sigh of relief. Scripture says that our faith is a gift from God, not a skill of our own mustering. God has already done the hard work of helping us please Him! We can exhaust ourselves trying to please the multitudes around us, but in Christ, there's only one to please, and that One is predictable. He is unchanging. His standards don't shift and bend depending on His moods or the shifting priorities of our culture. We seek to put a smile on His face not to earn brownie points or a spot next to Him—remember that He called us His friends! No, we do it simply because we're passionate about Him! We love Him and seek to please Him the same way we might seek to please a loved one. This is one of the essences of loving someone, no? To spend your life trying to put a smile on their face?

> *Do you realize that it is only in the gospel of Jesus Christ that you get the verdict before the performance? . . . You see, the verdict is in. And now I perform on the basis of the verdict. Because He loves me and He accepts me, I do not have to do things just to build up my résumé. I do not have to do things to make me look good. I can do things for the joy of doing them. I can help people to help people—not so I can feel better about myself, not so I can fill up the emptiness.*

TIMOTHY KELLER,
FROM *THE FREEDOM OF SELF FORGETFULNESS*

Having a heart for people, being able to read them instinctively, feeling empathy for where they are: these are superpowers, my friend. They are gifts, but they become curses when we turn them inward. When we use these gifts for our own purposes, we burn out. No, we must run our intentions through the filter of what Keller calls "blessed self-forgetfulness" or, as Paul put it: "Whatever you do, work heartily, as for the Lord and not for men" (Colossians 3:23 ESV). Let's embark on God-pleasing-people-pleasing. Let's focus on who gets the glory out of our giving. At every moment, I need to ask myself, who's being glorified here? Me or Him? If I keep my focus on bringing God glory, then I can give more selflessly—I can pull my foot off brake-hovering mode because their potential rejection of me doesn't hinder me from my goal of pleasing God.

> Because He loves me and He accepts me, I do not have to do things just to build up my résumé.

I can give more cheerfully, knowing that because of Jesus, I can never be rejected by the coolest, wisest, kindest, and all the -est's! And I can give confidently, knowing that because He is working in and through me, His purposes cannot be confounded by the strength or weakness of my giving.

When we reach the end of our hoarded resources,
Our Father's full giving has only begun. . . .
His love has no limit,
His grace has no measure,
His power has no boundary known unto men;
For out of His infinite riches in Jesus,
He giveth, and giveth and giveth again.
"HE GIVETH MORE GRACE" (HYMN)

I have never given someone a chocolate chip cookie and not been met by a big smile! I find they're the perfect gift, especially when they're still a little warm. These have a couple of secrets tucked into them: a pinch of cardamom, browned butter, and malted milk powder to give them a little extra nuttiness and chew.

Brown Butter Cardamom Chocolate Chip Cookies

ACTIVE TIME: 25 MINUTES | **TOTAL TIME**: 1 HOUR 10 MINUTES

14 tablespoons (7oz /198g) unsalted butter

½ teaspoon ground cardamom

½ cup (90g) granulated cane sugar

¾ cup (120g) packed dark brown sugar

1 teaspoon fine sea salt

2 teaspoons vanilla extract

2 large eggs, at room temperature

1¾ cups (250g) all purpose flour

½ teaspoon baking soda

5 tablespoons (1.6 oz, 45g) malted milk powder

2 3-ounce bars dark chocolate, chopped

Flaky salt for sprinkling

1. Adjust oven rack to middle position. Preheat oven to 375 degrees Fahrenheit. Line 3 sheet pans with parchment paper.

2. Set small heavy bottomed skillet over medium-high heat. Add 10 tablespoons of butter to the pan, and remaining 4 tablespoons butter in a large heatproof bowl; set the latter aside.

3. Heat the butter in the skillet until melted, then continue to cook, swirling the pan occasionally, until it turns golden brown and releases a nutty aroma. Stir in cardamom and remove from heat. Pour hot brown butter over the cold butter in bowl, and stir until completely melted. Set aside.

4. Whisk cane sugar, dark brown sugar, sea salt, and vanilla into the butter, whisking until smooth. Stir in eggs, then allow mixture to sit for 10 minutes, giving it a good whisk every couple of minutes to encourage the sugar to dissolve into the butter.

5. Meanwhile, whisk the flour, baking soda, and malted milk powder together in a medium bowl. Using a spatula, stir flour into wet ingredients until just combined. Stir in chocolate pieces, making sure they're well distributed.

6. Scoop 3-tablespoon portions onto lined sheet pan (a #24 scoop comes in handy here), 2 to 3 inches apart. Place only 6 portions on a baking sheet, as cookies will spread while baking. Sprinkle each portion with a little flaky salt.

7. Bake cookies, ideally one sheet at a time, until golden brown with set edges and soft centers, 13 to 15 minutes, rotating pans halfway through to ensure even cooking. Transfer sheet pan to wire rack to cool.

CHAPTER 44

When You Need Victory

I remember climbing to the top our rundown flat-roofed duplex in Culver City, California, in my twenties. The roof was warm under my bare feet from the day's sun, but my eyes were set on the giant sycamore tree that hung over our building. It felt like the closest I could get to God. Tears rolled down my face and I chronicled one injustice and heartbreak after another to Him, shaking my fist at Him, yelling and asking Him to intervene. I felt abandoned—I was getting pummeled by my opponent. *Just one small victory, Lord*, I said through tears and clenched teeth. *I just need one victory to keep me going.*

Life can feel like a constant battle. Whether the war rages within us or outside of us, it feels like its never-ending. And so there's a reason superhero and action movies are so popular. We all need a hero because the battle can feel too big for us to win on our own. We raise thought leaders, politicians, artists, teachers, and preachers, and put them in a position that no human can fully embody: that of a messiah, a savior, one who rides to victory on our behalf.

> Death is defeated. Eternity with God is ours.

The Israelites felt this on a deep level. Whether it was the Egyptians, the Babylonians, the Philistines (the list goes on an on), they were constantly under attack. And so it makes sense that the Old Testament Scriptures, especially the Psalms, repeatedly appealed to God to protect them from their enemies. God was the one who gave Joshua victory over Jericho, David victory over Goliath, Daniel victory over the lions, and yet it's clear that He didn't keep them from injury or at least temporary defeat.

> *Deliver me, O LORD, from evil men; preserve*
> *me from violent men, who plan evil things in*
> *their heart and stir up wars continually.*
> PSALM 140:1-2 ESV

But then David writes this:

> GOD the Lord, the strength of my salvation,
> You have covered my head in the day of battle.

PSALM 140:7 NASB

In Hebrew writing, the head signified the person themselves. God wasn't just protecting his head, but his whole being. The head was where blessing or calamity fell. David's head is protected; his enemies' heads may not enjoy the same benefit, and in fact, we know, spiritually speaking, that's true! Good has triumphed over evil in our own lives. Amen? Where we once were headed to an eternity separated from God, when we repent and accept Christ, good has pried us out of evil's strong grip. Death is defeated. Eternity with God is ours.

> Time is filled with swift transition
> Naught of earth unmoved can stand
> Build your hopes on things eternal
> Hold to God's unchanging hand!

SANDRA MCCRACKEN, "HOLD TO GOD'S UNCHANGING HAND"

I know eternity feels like a long ways off, right? Sometimes the victory promised to us on the other side of this reality feels intangible and abstract. It can sometimes feel like a dim trophy, because the oppression on this side of things is so painful. There is one thing that we can count on: in heaven, every battle we have waged here will be over. Healing, joy, and peace await us. Brendan, my husband, who suffers from ulcerative colitis, has had to contend with the possibility that he will not see healing in his lifetime on earth, that healing will only come when he passes over. Can we be humble enough to say that's enough? To take joy in that? Unlike so many spiritual teachers and gurus, Jesus didn't say we could escape suffering; instead He said suffering was almost guaranteed! Our solace is that our suffering here wouldn't be the final chapter in our story. Having overcome the world, and all its brokenness and pain, our heavenly existence will be filled with victory and rejoicing. The enemy doesn't get the last word!

> Christ has set us free to live a free life. So take your stand!
> Never again let anyone put a harness of slavery on you.

GALATIANS 5:1 THE MESSAGE

When we walk through our battlefields, scarred and on crutches, with a smile (however weak my friend; however weak) on our faces because our minds are set on the great feast that awaits us, it's not just strength to our bones. It's not just a way to keep ourselves from being confined once again to the lies that keep us in captivity. By believing in Jesus as the Son of God, we have a victory that overcomes:

For every child of God defeats this evil world, and
we achieve this victory through our faith.

I JOHN 5:4-5 NLT

Let's review. In Psalm 140, it states, "God the LORD, the strength of my salvation, You have covered my head in the day of battle" (Psalm 140:7 NASB). God protected David's head. But that doesn't mean he hadn't suffered injuries along the way; some of them were probably painful not only to his body but to his spirit too. They might have left him hobbling, discouraged, and disheartened. Psalm 140 was a reminder to David that despite it all, he was still standing! That's something we may need to remember when we feel like our opponent has gotten the best of us one too many times. We're still here, my friend! That is a victory in and of itself! I'm a bit of a mixed martial arts fan, and I can't tell you how many fights I've watched where a bloodied fighter, eye swollen, legs bruised who looks like he's going to lose, "miraculously" lands a wheel kick in the eleventh hour that knocks his opponent clean out. If you're standing, my friend, the battle is not over. And in fact, we know who wins the battle. He has won the battle already, darlin'. We just need to catch up to Him. Keep going.

> **Healing, joy, and peace await us.**

He will wipe away every tear from their eyes,
and death shall be no more, neither shall there
be mourning, nor crying, nor pain anymore,
for the former things have passed away.

REVELATION 21:4 ESV

Like the helmet on David's head, this *dum biryani* protects all the precious aromas of saffron, herbs, and spices in the pot so that they can be released at the table in all their victorious glory! Biryani is a layered dish that originates in India, but was inspired by the lavish rice dishes of the Persians. As you prepare the many layers, consider all the battles you have fought and overcome, by His grace, to get to this point today. Let that strengthen you for the battles you face now.

Chicken and Cranberry Biryani

MAKES 6-8 SERVINGS | **TOTAL TIME:** 2 HOURS 10 MINUTES | **ACTIVE TIME:** 1 HOUR 20 MINUTES

Cook's Note: Growing up, Mum only made biryani for special occasions. This is a simpler version, made even easier by using pre-packaged fried onions from South Asian stores—unlike those fried onions we put on our green bean casseroles at Thanksgiving, these have no batter. They're just pure fried onion goodness. You can fry your own: Thinly slice two yellow onions into half moons. Fry in about 2 cups of neutral oil until just starting to brown and remove with a slotted spoon to a paper towel–lined plate. Sprinkle with salt.

Rice:

1½ cups basmati rice

¼ cup warm (not hot!) whole milk

¼ teaspoon saffron threads

1 tablespoon kosher salt

1 tablespoon lemon juice

4 green cardamom pods, crushed (optional)

Chicken:

⅔ cup plain, full-fat Greek yogurt

¼ cup freshly squeezed lemon juice (about 1 lemon)

8 cloves garlic, grated on microplane

1 2-inch piece of ginger, grated on microplane

1 tablespoon sweet paprika

2 teaspoons ground coriander

2 teaspoons garam masala

1 teaspoon ground cumin

2 serrano peppers, either left whole or sliced in half (depending on how much heat you like)

1½ cups fried onions (see cook's note)

1½ pounds boneless, skinless chicken thighs, each sliced into 3 pieces

¼ cup ghee or avocado oil

¾ cup fresh mint leaves

¾ cup roughly chopped cilantro leaves and soft stems (coarse stems reserved and minced)

⅓ cup dried cranberries

1. Rinse the rice: pour rice into a large bowl and cover with water. Gently run your hands through the rice, being careful not to break the grains. The water should go cloudy as the rice releases excess starch. Drain, then repeat 2 to 3 times until the water runs clear. Cover once more with water, and allow to soak at room temperature for 30 to 45 minutes.

2. Make the saffron milk: drop saffron into warm milk. Cover and allow to steep for 30 minutes.

3. Marinate chicken: In a large, nonreactive bowl, stir together yogurt, lemon juice, garlic, ginger, paprika, coriander, garam masala, ground cumin, serrano peppers, 1½ tablespoons kosher salt and almost all of the fried onions (saving ½ cup for garnish). If you reserved and minced the coarse cilantro stems, add those to the marinade too. Add the chicken and massage well to coat. Cover and refrigerate.

4. Once rice has soaked, preheat oven to 400 degrees Fahrenheit.

5. Fill a large saucepan with 6 cups of water, 1 tablespoon kosher salt, 1 tablespoon lemon juice, and crushed cardamom pods. Set over high heat, cover, and bring to a boil.

6. Strain the rice, discarding the water, and tip into the boiling water. Stir and bring back up to the boil, then turn down to medium low and cook for 6 to 8 minutes, uncovered, until rice is cooked ¾ of the way through. Drain the rice through a colander, and spread out on a baking sheet to cool.

7. Set a large, heavy bottomed Dutch oven over medium-low heat and add the ghee or avocado oil. Add chicken, marinade, and ¼ cup water. Cook, stirring, to coat the chicken well for about 5 minutes, until warmed through. Turn off the heat.

8. Sprinkle half of the mint and cilantro over the top of the chicken, followed by 2 teaspoons of saffron milk.

9. Cover with half of the rice. Sprinkle half of remaining fried onions, and half of the cranberries. Repeat with remaining rice. Use a chopstick to poke 4-5 holes through the layers of rice. Drizzle remaining saffron milk over the top.

10. Sprinkle with remaining herbs, fried onions, and cranberries. Cover tightly with two layers of foil. Place over high heat for 2 to 3 minutes, until you can hear the contents of the pot sizzling. Put the lid on, bake for 35 to 45 minutes. Allow the biryani to cool, lid on, for about 10 minutes before serving. I like to bring it to the table with the lid on, then unveil it at the table so everyone can take in the aromas. Make sure you scoop all the way down to the bottom for each serving.

CHAPTER 45

When You Need Fruitfulness

This was the first year I planted a garden. I am the daughter, granddaughter, and great-granddaughter of farmers (maybe even further back than that) in India, and so I felt my very cells vibrate with knowledge when I ran my fingers through the soil. Whatever remnant I have of my ancestors in my DNA, they hummed with the sense that this is what is right!

At first my tomato plants stretched out gloriously, webbed leaves unfurling and turning toward the North Carolina sun. They seemed to grow inches overnight, and the marigolds I planted next to them kept the bugs away. Suddenly, things went sour. The marigolds went first, the proverbial canaries in the coal mine. The flowerhead blackened and drooped. The leaves browned and fell, until eventually all that was left was a little stump where the plant once stood. The tomatoes followed suit. New layers of branches came in decidedly differently than their siblings, each one ending in a gnarled, yellow fist. The leaves were thin and angry, like pursed lips. No longer did they stretch up towards the sky. Instead the stem started to stoop. And while it yielded a few tomatoes, they were few and far between, small and sour.

> God is the one who makes things grow. We cannot rush the process.

I found out I wasn't the only one experiencing this bout of fruitlessness. Many other gardeners across the South who had used the same soil faced the same pursed lips and gnarled fists in their beds. While we still don't know what happened, we suspect the soil may have been contaminated with some kind of herbicide, despite the soil company's most careful efforts to keep their soil as pure as possible. I am so disappointed that even though it's high time I pull everything out and start on the winter garden, I just can't bring myself to do it.

Are you experiencing this same disappointment and discouragement in your life, darling one? It can be so disheartening when we carefully plant and tend seeds we thought we were meant to cultivate, only to watch the soil every day for evidence of a shoot. We might question ourselves, might question God: should I keep going? Or should I stop? Worse still is when we look across to our friends and colleagues whose boughs are seemingly heavy with fruit. Why them and not me, Lord? What did I do wrong?

> *I planted the seed in your hearts, and Apollos watered it, but it was God who made it grow. It's not important who does the planting, or who does the watering. What's important is that God makes the seed grow.*
> I CORINTHIANS 3:6-7 NLT

In the gardens of our lives and projects, we can try to control everything from plant food to watering schedules, but ultimately, God is the one who makes things grow. We cannot rush the process—if the seed has been planted, and you are watering it with prayer, work, and attention, then only God can make it grow! In my own garden, not only have I seen perfect plants suddenly take a dive, but I've also seen plants revived from near death to super producers! God is the grower, not us. And so, we have to consult our planting schedule with Him. Just as you wouldn't plant tomato seeds in the winter (at least not in the Northern Hemisphere), sometimes the seeds we want to plant aren't appropriate for our current season. We must run our planting schedule by Him. If you're not seeing fruit right now, maybe you planted too early. You may need to take a break, and wait until He says, Yes the frost has passed! Plant them now!

God is always a few moves ahead of our opponent.

> *Unless the LORD builds a house, the work of the builders is wasted. Unless the LORD protects a city, guarding it with sentries will do no good.*
> PSALM 127:1 NLT

Similarly, we must ask the Lord to protect our garden. Every day I perused my garden for fungus, disease, or pests that sought to nibble at or destroy my plants. Sometimes our fruitlessness is the result of interruption or straight-up sabotage. God is always a few moves ahead of our opponent. When we move in lockstep with Him, not only do we ensure we're planting the right seeds, but we can also ensure that those seeds are protected and allowed to flourish.

Confession time: sometimes I'm made aware of my own fruitlessness by others' bounty! When they come excitedly to tell me about the success of their own gardens, while I try to be overjoyed for them, I can't help but look at my own branches, which seem limp and empty by comparison. But their fruit is not mine to bear. While I'm made to bear green zebra tomatoes, say, they're made to bear sweet peppers! I can no more bear their fruit than they can bear mine, and no amount of my tending the garden with extra plant food or pruning will make that happen! Trust the Gardener, darling. You are planted where you are, the way you are, for a reason. If He's the one that planted you, you will have no choice but to bear fruit!

When we spy fruit that wasn't intended for us, we can get jealous and impatient. We can want that fruit for our own. We can wonder whether our fruit will ever come to bear. But that fruit was intended for someone else to follow. It's their blessing. It wouldn't be right for our tree or for us.

What does Jesus say to us when we feel fruitless?

> *"Yes, I am the vine; you are the branches. Those who remain in Me, and I in them, will produce much fruit. For apart from Me you can do nothing."*
> JOHN 15:5 NLT

And did you catch that? For those of us growing out of the vine of Christ, we won't just bear fruit. We'll bear much fruit! Do we necessarily know what the fruit is? Not really, but we do know that the key to being fruitful lies in staying deeply rooted and connected to the vine. This is a mutually connected relationship where we can abide and rest in His presence! We must recognize that we are completely dependent on Him. Completely. There's nothing about our lives, our days, our very selves that doesn't come and go without His say-so.

The Lord is the consummate gardener, my friend, and we were made to bear fruit. He doesn't need to consult the seed packet or The Farmer's Almanac. He knows everything there is to know about your particular plant and what He needs to do to bear the sweetest, most abundant harvest from you. Rest in Him, darling. He's doing all the work whether you know it or not. The fruit is coming.

> *He is like a tree*
> *planted by streams of water*
> *that yields its fruit in its season,*
> *and its leaf does not wither.*
> *In all that he does, he prospers.*
> PSALM 1:3 ESV

Tomato Chaat Pie

MAKES 4 TO 5 SERVINGS | **ACTIVE TIME:** 25 TO 30 MINUTES | **TOTAL TIME:** 1 HOUR 15 MINUTES

1 7-ounce package refrigerated pie crust

Tamarind Chutney onions

2 tablespoons avocado oil

¾ large red onion, thinly sliced into half moons (165g, about 1¾ cups)

Kosher salt and freshly ground black pepper

¼ teaspoon ground cumin

1½ teaspoons tamarind concentrate

1 teaspoon dark brown sugar

Filling:

1 cup (about 115g) shredded mozzarella cheese

1 cup (about 100g) shredded cheddar cheese

½ cup mayo

½ cup minced mint

½ cup minced cilantro

2 tablespoons minced ginger

2 teaspoons lemon juice

1 teaspoon lemon zest

½ teaspoon chaat masala

½ teaspoon Aleppo pepper or red chili flake

4 medium tomatoes (heirloom or on-the-vine), sliced into ¼-inch thick slices

Extra virgin olive oil

1. Preheat oven to 375 degrees Fahrenheit. Keep one roll of pie dough on the counter, and allow it to sit for 15 minutes to take the chill off it.

2. Unroll pie dough into a 9-inch pie pan. Crimp edge with fingers. For best results, return to the refrigerator for 10 minutes.

3. Place a piece of parchment paper inside the pie pan and fill with pie weights or dried beans. Bake for 10 minutes. Then, remove parchment and pie weights/beans and bake another 10 minutes. Set aside to cool.

4. Make onions: heat oil over medium heat until shimmering. Sprinkle in onions along with a pinch of salt. Cook until just starting to brown. Add a splash of water, and scrape up any brown bits that may be stuck to the pan. Add cumin and black pepper and cook for 30 seconds.

5. Turn heat down to low. Add tamarind concentrate, brown sugar, and another big splash of water. Stir well and cook for another minute until water has been absorbed and onions look jammy. Remove from heat.

6. Set tomatoes on paper towel–lined plate. Sprinkle with a little salt on each side. Let them sit for 10 minutes.

7. Mix filling ingredients together in a medium bowl with a little glue of olive oil until well combined. Taste for seasoning!

8. Assemble pie: scoop cheese mixture into the pie and smooth out. Spread onions on top of the cheese mixture. Finally, lay tomatoes on top in a circle, overlapping them a little. Drizzle each tomato with a little olive oil, and then bake for 30 to 40 minutes, rotating the pie halfway through to ensure even cooking. Allow to cool for 10 minutes before you slice into it!

CHAPTER 46

When You Need Grace

W ould you do me a favor?

I have, just so you know, defaced your home with insulting graffiti. I've stolen your outgoing mail and rewritten the words therein. Woops! Oh, and I've eaten all the cookies I could find in your cabinets and, oh! Those dishes in the sink? I won't be washing those.

So . . . about that favor. I could really use a ride to the airport. Would you mind?

Imagine you were on the receiving end of this request. I don't know about you, but my response would run something along the lines of: "Get out of here and be thankful I don't call the cops!"

But what if I said "yes." That, my friends, would be grace.

Grace, biblically, is defined as "unmerited favor."

Let's be real here: Grace doesn't make a ton of logical sense. It appears to fly in the face of how we understand justice, in the absolute sense. And if there's anyone who stands for justice, it's God, right? After all, He is the supreme-ist of Supreme Judges. We see this office attributed to Him time and again, from Genesis . . .

> *Will not the Judge of all the earth do right?*
> GENESIS 18:25 NIV

. . . to Revelation.

> *And I saw the dead, great and small, standing before the throne, and books were opened. . . . The dead were judged according to what they had done as recorded in the books.*
> REVELATION 20:12 NIV

We can stomp through the many hallways of His magnificent palace, all the way to the foot of His marvelous throne!

The Hebrew word used for God's grace is *channun*, a word uniquely applicable to God. It means "inclining to the cry of the vexed debtor." In the judgment paradigm, it's listening and responding with patience and mercy to someone God has no reason to respond to that way! The debtor is vexed because he does indeed owe God a debt. The plaintiff is indeed guilty. And yet He shows us grace because He is indeed gracious. Both perfect justice and perfect grace are in His nature.

> All of God's justice was poured out on Jesus, burying our debt in Jesus' death.

I think of grace sometimes when I'm making a vinaigrette, a deceptively simple thing to make because you're forcing together two elements that don't like to play together, oil and vinegar! I was in charge of salads at Lucques, an incredible restaurant in Los Angeles that was known for its fresh, seasonal fare. The key to bringing them together is to slowly, patiently whisk the oil into the vinegar, but wouldn't you know it, whenever Chef was in the kitchen, that's when mine "broke" and I'd have to start all over again, wasting both precious product and time. And so, in my own kitchen, how grateful am I for emulsifiers like mustard and honey! They cover a multitude of vinaigrette-making sins, persuading the frenemies known as oil and vinegar to play nice even if the cook (me) hasn't done a good job of whisking the oil into the vinegar.

So if we're feeling as broken as my vinaigrettes, what should we do?

> *Come boldly to the throne of grace, that we may obtain*
> *mercy and find grace to help in time of need.*
> HEBREWS 4:16 NKJV

We need to hear this, beloved. If you need grace, come and get it!

God doesn't hide His grace behind a fortress. We don't need to scale a great wall or walk into His courts stooped over so we don't make eye contact. The doors are open, the guards are commanded to stand down, our name's on the list. We, His children, can stomp through the many hallways of His magnificent palace, barefoot and maybe a little disheveled, all the way to the foot of His marvelous throne! There, we're invited to look Him right in the eye and ask for what we need—grace, mercy, forgiveness, even help to overcome the debt we've accrued. Our pockets may be empty. Our hearts may be ashamed. But the truth is we don't come with anything worthy to pay our debt, nothing to establish the basis for our deserving. And yet, not only does He say come, but come boldly! Come without shame! The perfect judge, whom we owe, whom we've disgraced and insulted and flaunted what He gave us while He, long-suffering, hadn't yet come to rightly collect . . . He's the one who says, Come boldly to Me. Wow!

Doesn't something in us both exult and cringe? This sounds great. It also sounds . . . uncomfortable. It's like being invited to a smashingly fun party, when you're wearing your gym-then-gardening clothes, by someone you just publicly mocked on social media (and they liked the post so you know they saw it). The contradictory nature of God's grace is really good news. But it's hard to take. In a way, it can almost make us feel worse! It's like "AND you're being nice to me?"

This is where Jesus comes in. We don't feel worthy (because we're not worthy) to receive God's grace (instead of His justice). We are vexed debtors. But Jesus is not. He doesn't owe God any payback because, as He is God and lived a sinless life, He accrued no such debt. Yet Jesus paid off debt anyway. Not His but ours, yours, and mine. All of God's justice was poured out on Jesus, burying our debt in Jesus' death. This was God's ultimate grace plan from the beginning. To our great benefit. We don't deserve it. In Christ we get it. Nothing to brag about. Everything to celebrate.

> We don't deserve it. In Christ we get it. Nothing to brag about. Everything to celebrate.

> *For it is by grace you have been saved, through faith–and this is not from yourselves, it is the gift of God– not by works, so that no one can boast.*
> EPHESIANS 2:8-9 NIV

And so, if you need grace, darling, go and get it. It's yours for the taking. In the meantime, I'll go do your dishes now, okay?

No-Fail Vinaigrette

TOTAL TIME: 10 MINUTES | **ACTIVE TIME:** 10 MINUTES

3 tablespoons freshly squeezed lemon juice (about 1 lemon)

3 tablespoons unseasoned rice wine vinegar

¼ cup finely minced shallot

1 teaspoon dijon mustard

2 teaspoons honey

¾ cup extra virgin olive oil

Kosher salt and freshly ground black pepper

1. Whisk together lemon juice and rice wine vinegar in a medium bowl. Add the shallots, season with a big pinch of salt, and allow to sit for 5 minutes.

2. Now add dijon mustard and honey. Whisk together.

3. Slowly pour extra virgin olive oil, in a thin stream, while whisking constantly until you get a silky vinaigrette. Season with salt and pepper. To make sure your dressing is properly seasoned, draw a piece of lettuce through the vinaigrette. Take a bite, and adjust seasoning accordingly. Store in an air-tight jar, and store in the fridge for 3 to 4 days (bring to room temperature before you use it!).

CHAPTER 47

When You Need Joy

The past few years have drained my joy. We bid adieu to our hometown of twenty years. The reemergence of a health issue we believed long-buried tested our faith. Breaks in a decade-long friendship have left me cautious about new ones. I look back at my joy with longing, but also skepticism: good things don't last forever.

This is a hard thing to admit, my friend. By all accounts, the thing y'all respond to when you watch me on TV or social media is my joy! If my joy tank continues to leak, then what do I share with you all?

And yet, when I look a little closer over the years since the Good Lord called me by name, I realize that there has always been one thing or another sapping my joy. Family catastrophes, financial struggles, even two bouts of postpartum depression. Through it all, whenever I got to communicate with you all, a genuine joy overtook me. What you've seen over the years is real—as I always tell my husband, I'm a journalist by training, not an actor. I can't fake it. So, where does that joy come from? Let's figure it out.

Much of creation is still a source of great joy: the soaring cliffs and majestic ocean of Big Sur, California; a baby laughing so hard she nearly loses her breath . . . If we have eyes to see it, joy is God's bailiwick.

> Every mile we cross, every year that goes by, brings us closer to the place of joy unlimited.

Joy is the serious business of heaven.
C. S. LEWIS

The Bible talks of a joy built on a certain future, where the tension within us is resolved. Waiting on that joy is, in and of itself, part of the joy. The Israelites wandered in the wilderness empowered by the joy awaiting them in the promised land of milk and honey. The angel announced Jesus' birth to the shepherds with rejoicing over what He'd do for them in the future. Today, we wait with anticipation for His return when all will be made right in the world and in our hearts.

*"So you have sorrow now, but I will see you again; then you
will rejoice, and no one can rob you of that joy."*
JOHN 16:22 NLT

If you've ever journeyed on I-95 between North and South Carolina, then you might understand this anticipation of joy, in the unlikely form of a pitstop named "South of the Border." This larger-than-life roadside attraction is as massive as it is loud, its faux-Mexican theme informing the design of the two-hundred-foot high Sombrero Observation tower, the Hot Tamale restaurant, and yes, even a Reptile Lagoon! This year, my husband told the girls that on our way back from our spring break trip to Charleston, South Carolina, we'd stop. The girls screamed with joy. About one hundred miles before South of the Border, the billboards began. A hand-drawn flamingo cried, "You'll be tickled pink! South of the Border. 31 miles!" Another says, "World's Number One Miniature Golf! 16 miles!" Still another, bedecked with a giant hot dog, declares, "You never sausage a place! 2 miles!"

With every sign, the girls yelled louder, the anticipation building until they were fit to burst! They were filled with joy even though they weren't there yet, because their destination was assured. Every sign of their impending arrival only increased their joy! Do you see how this mirrors our own experience as travelers on The Way? The journey may be arduous, but we keep our eyes peeled for the signs, and those signs cause us to rejoice. And when we reach the exit ramp, we rejoice even more because we get to exit here, by no effort of our own!

> If I set Him as the filler of my joy tank, it will never run dry because He never runs dry.

The joy of the Lord is our strength. What is this joy? It's the joy not of the past nor the present but in the future! It's the joy of anticipating a reality that's both now and also not yet. And it's that joy that strengthens us through the trials we're embroiled in. Much like the wait for South of the Border—every mile we cross, every year that goes by, brings us closer to the place of joy unlimited.

When we lose our joy, we lose sight of our hope. When we lose sight of hope, we lose our hold on faith. We might even walk away from our relationship with God. I don't want to overspiritualize, but if there is an enemy of our souls, stealing our joy would be an easy Jenga tile to pull. How do we protect our joy?

UNWIND

I have set the LORD continually before me;
Because He is at my right hand, I will not be shaken.
Therefore my heart is glad and my glory rejoices.
You will make known to me the way of life;
In Your presence is fullness of joy;
In Your right hand there are pleasures forever.

PSALM 16:8-9, 11 NASB

The writer set the Lord in front of him as he scanned the horizon. Think of how an Instagram filter changes the way we see ourselves. On a much more profound level, looking at the world through the lens of Christ allows us to properly assess our lives. How does this present trial stack up against the promise we have in Him? In His presence is not just joy, but the fullness of joy—in Hebrew, the word used indicates satiety. His is the joy that fills us to the brim and will never run dry. It overwhelms our sadness and washes away discouragement. When it feels like there's so much brokenness that there's no room for joy, this joy reminds us that He is a banquet, an all you can eat! If I set Him as the filler of my joy tank, it will never run dry because He never runs dry. That means I will always have joy not just to strengthen my walk, but to share with you all. And it isn't any run-of-the-mill joy. This is the good stuff, the creme de la creme, VIP joy, the kind that can only come as a gift from the Holy Spirit. This is the joy that is available to you and to me, beloved. Set Him before you. Look for the signs. And enjoy the ride. Our exit is coming soon!

> I will always have joy not just to strengthen my walk, but to share with you all.

I. Love. Potatoes. That creamy, fluffy starch that readily absorbs nearly any flavor you throw at it? Or the crispy snap of a fried potato? What about the gentle bounce and chew of a potato dumpling? Potatoes are oh-so flexible, and oh-so ready to please, which is why they fill me with so much joy. One of my favorite preparations hails from the town of my birth, Bombay: It's a simple enough preparation, gilded in turmeric, cumin seeds, lots of lemon juice, and cilantro. But that combination fills my heart with joy. What could be better? Using prepackaged gnocchi, and finishing it with a shower of Parmesan cheese. Yeah. That's better.

Bombay Gnocchi

ACTIVE TIME: 20 TO 25 MINUTES | **TOTAL TIME:** 25 MINUTES

1 1-pound package gnocchi

¼ cup ghee + 2 teaspoons extra

¾ teaspoons black or brown mustard seeds

¾ teaspoons cumin seeds

1 serrano or jalapeño chili, minced (seeds and membranes removed if you don't like heat)

¼ teaspoon turmeric

½ teaspoon lemon juice

1½ teaspoons sugar

¼ cup minced cilantro

Kosher salt and freshly ground black pepper

Freshly grated Parmesan cheese

1. Bring a large pot of water to a boil. Season the water with enough salt that it tastes like ocean water. Add the gnocchi and cook to package directions. Remove gnocchi with a spider or slotted spoon to a paper towel-lined sheet pan. Save about ½ cup of gnocchi water.

2. Place a large skillet over medium high heat. Warm ghee on medium-high heat until it shimmers. Add mustard seeds and cumin seeds. Allow them to sizzle for a few seconds, then add the gnocchi. Toss well to coat, and cook, without moving too often until they start to turn crisp and golden brown, about 6 to 7 minutes.

3. Move gnocchi to the perimeter of the pan. Add extra ghee to the center of the pan, and add green chili and turmeric. Pull gnocchi back to the middle of the pan, and coat in the seeds, chili, and turmeric. Cook, stirring and flipping the gnocchi frequently, about 1 minute.

4. Sprinkle with lemon juice, sugar, and cilantro. Toss to coat very well. Finish with a last sprinkle of salt and pepper, and parmesan if desired. Serve immediately!

CHAPTER 48

When You Need Community

The pandemic confirmed what I'd always suspected: I'm an extrovert. I watched as members of my extended family, who are more introverted, flourished; this was the kind of isolation they'd always dreamed of! Their lives didn't change much except that now, no one expected any social activity out of them. Bliss!

But I felt my spirit shrivel up, starved for nutrition. While social congress exhausts them, it energizes me. My girls were the same, rushing over to any child we saw in public, and finding something to compliment about them, hoping it would strike up a conversation. We are people-people in our family!

Whether you're an introvert or an extrovert, community is commanded by Scripture.

And let us consider how to stir up one another to love and good works, not neglecting to meet together, as is the habit of some, but encouraging one another, and all the more as you see the Day drawing near.
HEBREWS 10:24-25 ESV

The author wrote to a community of Hebrews who, under threat of persecution, were tempted to cast away their faith in Christ. This bit of background underscores just how important gathering is; even in times of persecution, the author thought it more dangerous to reject meeting! Why?

Gathering strengthens our faith.

Gathering strengthens our faith. When we aren't in community, our faith becomes more theoretical than practical. When iron doesn't sharpen iron, it goes dull, and eventually useless. So too with our walk, dear introverted friend. Even if it's just once a week, and even if you need a nap afterward because it draws from your tank, I urge you to go to church or to whatever Jesus-centered gathering you can. Nothing could be more of a threat to our faith than isolation, even persecution.

Created by a relational God, we are created for relationship both with Him and with others. Whether you're a follower of Christ or not, we all have a longing to be better: more loving, more patient, more charitable, braver, bolder, wiser. The author of this verse implies that the key to this leveling up is to be "stirred up"—this makes me think of whipping cream. Stick with me. I know. I'm weird.

Unwhipped, it's thick and creamy and sure, quite a lovely blanket over a bowl of fresh strawberries. But, oh, take a whisk to it . . . those metal balloons beating air between the fat molecules transform it into quite something else . . . delicate clouds of ethereal bliss that melt on the tongue! The pathway to love and good works, says the author of Hebrews, is to be whipped up. And the pathway to being whipped up? You guessed it, community. While solitude is the best backdrop for, say, meditating on the Word, or communing with Him, the best way to practice love and good works is to practice on others! This is the best motivation to push through when the first few meetings are awkward and maybe a bit discouraging. Keep going. Even when you whip cream, you have to start slowly.

Hopefully I've convinced those of you who avoid community to seek it and reaffirmed my fellow extroverts that we're craving a good thing! And not just in a self-serving way! We seek out community not necessarily just to fill our cup, but to find ways to fill other's cups too.

> The best way to practice love and good works is to practice on others!

But what do you do if community is hard to find? Build it yourself.

When I started to pour myself into cooking, community came with it in pretty short order. Offer to cook someone a meal, and more often than not, they'll say, What time should I be there?

Breaking bread knits souls together because it's the supernatural way of things. God shared a meal with the elders of Israel (Exodus 24:9–11) as a way to seal His covenant with them. Jesus is often found reclining at the table. We repeat His last supper with our spiritual family as a reminder of the central belief that holds us together. And of course, we all look forward to the tremendous wedding feast that awaits us when we're all reunited with Him (just so you know, I will be eating seconds, thirds, and fourth helpings that day, don't judge me).

There's a shimmer of the sacred glimmering through something as mundane as eating together. If it matters in heaven, it matters down here. So, if you need community, build it! If you build it, they will come! I know this to be true. Commit to breaking bread with someone once a week. Put it in the calendar. It can be as simple as bagels and coffee or as complex as a full Sichuan-style feast. I've done both, and both have fed me and my guests, body and spirit.

> Breaking bread knits souls together because it's the supernatural way of things.

I leave you with one of my favorite brunch dishes, Persian Spinach and Eggs, also known as Nargissi. Nargissi refers to the narcissus flower, named after the mythical Greek character who was so enamored with himself that upon catching a glimpse of his visage in a pool of water, stared at himself until he died. In his place sprouted the flower. What a good reminder to ourselves that community draws our eyes away from ourselves, and onto others and Himself. Let us not forsake gathering, my brothers and sisters, for our own sake, and for the sake of those God made us to bless!

Nargissi: Persian Spinach and Eggs

MAKES 2 TO 4 SERVINGS | **TOTAL TIME:** 30 MINUTES | **ACTIVE TIME:** 30 MINUTES

3 tablespoons extra virgin olive oil

2 medium leeks, white and light green parts only, sliced into ¼-inch half moons (about 2 cups)

2 cloves garlic, minced

½ teaspoon ground turmeric

1 to 1.5 pounds raw spinach leaves, trimmed of stalks, rinsed (anywhere from 2 to 4 bunches, depending on the size of the bunches)

Salt and pepper

A little freshly grated nutmeg

Zest and juice of ½ large lemon

Zest and juice of ¼ large orange

Pinch of saffron, infused into 1 tablespoon hot water

4 large chicken eggs

1. Set a large skillet over medium heat. Add the oil and once it's shimmering, add the leeks and garlic. Sprinkle with a little salt and pepper. Stir frequently until softened and aromatic, and just the tiniest bit golden brown.

2. Add the turmeric and stir constantly, about 30 seconds.

3. Now add the spinach, a little at a time. Toss, covering the whole spinach leaves in the turmeric-scented aromatics. Cover, and allow to cook for 30 seconds, then uncover and add the next batch. Toss, cover, and repeat until all the spinach has been added and has wilted. Season with a little salt, pepper, and freshly grated nutmeg.

4. Now add the citrus zest and juice, along with the saffron tea. Stir well. Allow some of the liquid to evaporate.

5. Make four indentations, and crack an egg into each one. Season each egg with salt and pepper. Turn the heat down to medium low and cook for 3 to 7 minutes depending on how you like your eggs. Serve immediately with warm flatbread.

CHAPTER 49

When You Need
Contentment

I taught myself to cook because I wasn't content.

You see, my mum kept cookies, cake, and ice cream to a minimum. She was concerned for our health, particularly mine since I was a little portly when I was little. One day I realized that while there was a shortage of treats in the house, there was plenty of flour, sugar, and butter, not to mention hundreds of my mum's favorite cookbooks! Thus began the weekend ritual of waiting until my parents took a nap, and then whipping up a flurry of scones, cookies, and cakes. By the time they'd arisen from their slumber, I'd scarfed down more than my fair share of whatever I'd made, hurrying before one parental unit or the other would say, "Aaru! That's enough!"

Thus was my confidence in the kitchen and my love for cooking born: out of greed. Ha!

These days, I still struggle with contentment. Whether it's parenting, my skills in the kitchen, my body, my career, I always want more.

Contentment? Do you mean how much abundance will make me happy?!

How in the world am I ever supposed to know how much is enough? I can't trust myself. I've eaten until I was in physical pain. I've exercised until I injured myself. I've drunk until . . . well, let's just say I know more than one hangover cure. And yet I still don't always know my limit! I know I've often lived as the leech:

> *The leech has two daughters: Give and Give.*
> PROVERBS 30:15 ESV

Ouch. Let's keep reading that proverb to see if it gets any better.

> *Three things are never satisfied; four that*
> *never say, "Enough": Sheol, the barren*
> *womb, the land never satisfied with water,*
> *and fire that never says, "Enough."*
> PROVERBS 30:15–16 ESV

Oh, what a picture of discontentment. And what a picture of how our constant seeking for more, our "never enough," steals life from us. Sheol is the place of death, the wages for sin, the source of the darkness that aims to swallow up the sweetness of God's grace in our lives. The barren womb is a place where life is hoped for but doesn't grow; this is me when all I can see is the unfulfilled hopes in my life. The drought-ridden land that never gets enough water reminds me of how, no matter how much God gives me, I'm always asking for more. And the fire, the eater of tinder— what a picture of my greed, gorging myself on more and more fuel, but never being satisfied. All of these examples conjure up images of death, perhaps because to chase contentment, to have but never have enough, is not life-giving. Perhaps that abyss that lies within all of us, the one that cries out to be filled, to be content, is not meant to be filled with the things of this world. Nothing is big enough, deep enough, or profound enough.

May you have the power to understand, as all God's people should,
how wide, how long, how high, and how deep His love is.
EPHESIANS 3:18 NLT

Our craving for contentment is actually a craving for Him, His love. That's why nothing here can satisfy, because it was never meant to. The things of this world are good, don't get me wrong! I take so much joy in a good chocolate chip cookie, in my daughters' laughter, in the arms of my husband. But they will never gratify me as fully, completely, or as long-lastingly as He does. Chasing the things of this world for contentment leads to death of the soul. Chasing Him leads to life.

In this way, we can be content even if we have nothing. We, children of the Giver of life, are called to be gratified with life. Paul's words to the Philippians are a bold statement of his focus on life over death in every moment, even in prison. Far from friends, far from comfort in nearly every easily identifiable way, yet he says,

> Chasing the things of this world for contentment leads to death of the soul. Chasing Him leads to life.

I have learned to be content regardless of my circumstances. I know how
to live humbly, and I know how to abound. I am accustomed to any and
every situation—to being filled and being hungry, to having plenty and
having need. I can do all things through Christ who gives me strength.
PHILIPPIANS 4:11-13 BSB

Contentment is Holy Spirit business. This is God business. This is the business of Christ who gives you strength. And we will need strength for this because our bodies will cry out for the quick fix, for the immediate high of earthly contentment. We need the Holy Spirit to give us eyes to see what we do have, ears to hear the good in every circumstance. If we see and seek Christ, if we hear and obey Christ, contentment is ours because in Him, we have enough. In Him, we are enough. Death has no hold on you, if you are in the Resurrected One, so, dear heart, you don't have to keep your eyes on the things of death anymore. You can look around at any situation and know that all of this always was temporary to begin with. This too shall pass. All but Christ shall pass.

> *But seek first the kingdom of God and his righteousness,*
> *and all these things will be added to you.*
> MATTHEW 6:33 ESV

Of all the hundreds of curries I've eaten in my life, this one is my favorite, hands down. I crave it. As someone who has grown up away from home for her entire life, the flavors of home hold a deep significance. The combination of curry leaves, coconut, and a spice blend heavy on black peppercorns—oh, those are the hallmarks of my hometown, Mangalore. The thing about contentment is that we feel like only when we get that *one* thing we're craving will we be content. And often, that's not wholly true. When I get a craving for home though, this is what does it for me. This curry. May you find contentment in it too!

We can be content even if we have nothing.

Mangalorean Beef Curry with Coconut, Curry Leaf, and Black Peppercorns (Beef Sukka)

MAKES 6 SERVINGS | **TOTAL TIME:** 1 HOUR 15 MINUTES | **ACTIVE TIME:** 1 HOUR

Pronounced "SOOK-kah" this is my very favourite curry from my hometown of Mangalore, India. Unlike most other curries you may have tried, this one has very little gravy. It's what we call a "dry curry" that's wonderful eaten with either plain white rice, or the everyday whole wheat flatbreads that we call chapati. Don't be intimated by all the ingredients. Think of it as three steps: make the masala, cook the meat, finish the dish with the spiced sizzling oil. This dish is worth the effort and definitely celebration-worthy!

Masala

8 dried red chilis, such as guajillo or Kashmir

2 tablespoons coriander seeds

1½ teaspoons cumin seeds

2-inch piece of cinnamon

8 black peppercorns

6 whole cloves

1 tablespoon white basmati rice

1 sprig curry leaves (about 15 leaves)

1 teaspoon black or brown mustard seeds

1 teaspoon ground turmeric

2 marble-sized balls of seedless tamarind pulp (about 20g)

Curry

1 medium yellow onion (200g), thinly sliced into half moons

1 to 2 serrano or jalapeño chilis, sliced in half lengthwise (seeds and membranes removed if you don't like spicy food)

1-inch thumb ginger, finely chopped

6 cloves garlic, thinly sliced

2 pounds beef chuck roast, trimmed of thick fat, cut into ¾-inch cubes

Kosher salt

Tadka (finishing spiced oil)

3 tablespoons coconut or avocado oil

5 cloves garlic, crushed

1 teaspoon black or brown mustard seeds

2 sprigs fresh curry leaves (about 30 leaves)

1 small yellow onion (150g), thinly sliced into half moons

1¾ cup grated fresh or frozen coconut (or ¾ cup unsweetened dried coconut)

¼ cup fresh cilantro leaves for garnish

1. Make masala: Warm a small skillet over medium-low heat, and toast each of the spices (except the turmeric), individually, until they give off a fragrant aroma. When toasting the curry leaves, cook until they crisp up slightly. Tip all the spices onto a plate to cool. Add the turmeric to the plate. Grind to a fine powder. Add this masala to a blender along with tamarind balls and 1 cup of water. Grind to a smooth paste and set aside.

2. Place beef, masala paste, sliced onion, green chilis, ginger, and garlic in a large, heavy-bottomed Dutch oven. Stir in 2 teaspoons of kosher salt. Cover, and heat over a medium-high flame until the mixture starts to sizzle healthily, then turn the heat down to medium-low, and cook for 7 minutes, stirring every now and then. Cook for another 7 minutes uncovered, continuing to stir occasionally, until meat is tender and a gravy has formed.

3. Heat a large kadhai, wok, or cast iron skillet over medium high heat. Add the oil and garlic cloves, and cook until garlic is golden brown.

4. Add the mustard seeds; they will start to sizzle and pop. Now add the curry leaves and onions—the pan might sizzle furiously so arm yourself with a lid! Once the fury has subsided, remove the lid and cook, stirring often, until onions have turned golden brown.

5. Sprinkle in the coconut, and sauté until golden flecks develop. Now carefully add the beef curry and sauté, letting some (not all) of the gravy evaporate. If you can get a delicate crust on the beef too, that's great! Taste for seasoning, finishing with salt, pepper, and a flurry of fresh cilantro leaves.

CHAPTER 50

When You Need Freedom

We live in a world that holds "Freedom!" up as one of the highest ideals of mankind. It's not only in our national anthem but also our beer commercials, our campaign slogans . . . Freedom is popular in American advertising of all sorts. It's cross-cultural too! Freedom is on the hearts and minds of folks at a monster truck rally and a pride parade, a summer music festival and a political party convention, on the lips of a screaming teenager and a lecturing octogenarian.

Arguably though, this was not always so. In the ancient world, the world of Scripture, sovereigns reigned over tribes, cities, city-states, and nations. The good of society was a bigger priority than the good of the individual. God or "the gods" reigned above humanity. It was assumed that someone else had better be in charge because if there were this many wars at the whimsies of these few kings, queens, and emperors, how many more would there be if every person of earth were given a crown?

> Freedom is a matter of whom or what we are bound by.

Against this backdrop, the words of Christ seem far less provocative than they may appear to us now.

> *Jesus answered them, "Truly, truly, I say to you,*
> *everyone who practices sin is a slave to sin."*
> JOHN 8:34 ESV

Wow. Let's remember that Jesus said this to Jews, those who had suffered an infamous history of slavery: to the Egyptians for twenty generations, around three generations to the Babylonians, and at that moment, under colonial rule of the Romans for almost five generations. This was a risky play, Jesus! But, being divine in nature, Jesus wasn't speaking in earthly terms, but in heavenly ones. Freedom, then, is a matter of whom or what we are bound by. So, if you need freedom today the question is not only "freedom from what" but also, necessarily, "what is keeping your heart captive"?

I don't always sense my freedom in the present, but I always see it in hindsight.

Wait a second, Aarti, I hear you say. Didn't our heavenly Father promise us freedom!? Didn't He say:

> It is for freedom that Christ has set us free. Stand firm, then, and do not let yourselves be burdened.
> GALATIANS 5:1 NIV

And . . .

> Now the Lord is the Spirit, and where the Spirit of the Lord is, there is freedom.
> II CORINTHIANS 3:17 NIV

Love, you aren't wrong! Buuuuttt . . .

Freedom from what? Freedom from sin! Any promise of freedom that isn't rooted in this true freedom is merely slavery-to-sin redecorated. Or, as Peter wrote:

> They promise them freedom, but they themselves are slaves of corruption. For whatever overcomes a person, to that he is enslaved.
> II PETER 2:19 ESV

When you need freedom, running deeper into captivity would be the worst possible outcome. So how do we know which way we're running? We must examine where that path leads, because that will reveal whom we're serving. I have found so often that choosing His way has meant not choosing my way. It can feel like handcuffs in the short term. But in the long term, I've always been able to look back and see how His way allowed me to avoid all kinds of pitfalls, hurdles, and complications. I don't always sense my freedom in the present, but I always see it in hindsight. He is a trustworthy and good Father. Christ came to set us free from the slavery of sin, and that is the best true freedom we could ever have. As Christ Himself said:

> "The Spirit of the Lord is upon me,
> because he has anointed me
> to proclaim good news to the poor.
> He has sent me to proclaim liberty to the captives
> and recovering of sight to the blind,
> to set at liberty those who are oppressed,
> to proclaim the year of the Lord's favor."
> LUKE 4:18-19 ESV (SEE ALSO ISAIAH 61:1-2.)

I'm sure there's a connection to be made between salmon and the freedom they feel to swim upstream, how they literally go against the flow in order to satisfy their biological imperative. Sometimes, for us to gain true freedom, it can feel like we're fighting against

He is a trustworthy and good Father.

ourselves! I could go on with this metaphor. But honestly? I just love this recipe and the freedom it gives me in the kitchen when I know there are a lot of mouths to feed. One side of salmon, in the fridge for an hour, and then in the oven for about 10 minutes and we're done! AND it's beautiful?! Yes!!

Roasted Salmon
with Table-side Tadka

ACTIVE TIME: 35 MINUTES | **TOTAL TIME:** 1 HOUR 45 MINUTES TO 1 HOUR, 55 MINUTES

2 teaspoons fennel seeds, divided

Kosher salt

1 2½-pound skin-on side of salmon, pin bones removed and belly fat trimmed, uniformly thick from end to end if possible

1½ tablespoons honey

Avocado oil spray

3 tablespoons ghee

3 tablespoons extra virgin olive oil

1 teaspoon nigella seeds (or cumin seeds)

1 tablespoon (about 2-inch thumb) minced ginger

1 jalapeño or serrano chili, minced (remove seeds and membranes if you prefer less heat)

4 to 5 scallions, white and green parts sliced thinly on the diagonal, divided

1 lemon, sliced into wedges

1. Grind 1 teaspoon fennel seeds to a fine powder (set remaining 1 teaspoon fennel seeds aside for later). Mix fennel powder with 2 teaspoons kosher salt. Place salmon, skin-side down, on a sheet pan or dish, and sprinkle fennel salt evenly over the fish. Refrigerate, uncovered, for 1 hour.

2. Position your oven rack about 7 inches from the broiler element.

3. Pull the salmon from your fridge, and pat it dry with some paper towels to mop up any moisture on the surface of the fish. Brush the surface evenly with honey.

4. Line a sheet pan with parchment paper and lightly cover in cooking spray. Transfer the salmon, skin side down, to the sheet pan. Slide into the oven, and cook under the broiler for 8 to 10 minutes, until salmon is lightly browned.

5. Remove salmon from the oven. Set your oven to 250 degrees Fahrenheit.

6. Check the temperature of the center of the salmon; if it registers 125 degrees Fahrenheit, you're all done and you can turn the oven off; you're done! If not, then roast for 5 to 10 minutes (depending on the thickness of your salmon) until it reaches 125 degrees Fahrenheit in the center.

7. Transfer cooked salmon to your platter while you make the tadka.

8. To make the tadka, warm ghee and olive oil in a medium skillet until it shimmers.

9. Add remaining 1 teaspoon of fennel seeds along with nigella seeds. Cook for 30 seconds, allowing the fennel seeds to deepen in color a little, then quickly add ginger, jalapeño, and scallion whites. Season with a big pinch of salt, and sauté until they soften, about 1 minute. Add the scallion greens. Pour the sizzling oil over the salmon at the table for a big presentation! Squeeze a couple of wedges of lemon over the top. Dinner (and a show) is served!

Acknowledgments

There were myriad moments when I thought I'd never finish this book.

The fact that I did is in great part due to my husband, Brendan. He picked me up when I was exhausted, swatted away the fog of lies that told me I couldn't do it, and literally helped me write devotionals when I fell behind. I ran every word and every bite in this book past him because his wisdom and his palate are unmatched. He took on the lion's share of parenting duties too: lunchboxes, movie nights, massaging sore bellies . . . He even planned all their Christmas presents because my bandwidth was too full. He was husband, father, mother, writer, theologian, and recipe evaluator, with nary a complaint. I couldn't have done this without you, Baba. I thank God that you were playing Tori Amos so loudly the day I walked by your dorm room (I still think you play music too loudly). You're a never-ending gift to me. Thank you.

To our daughters, Eliyah and Moses: you sacrificed a lot of time with your mama over the past few months. I know how hard that was on you, especially when I missed Christmas. You cheered me on when I was tired. You shared your thoughts on my food. When you two tell me it's good, it means more to me that you might ever know. I'm so proud that I get to be your mum. I love you so much. Thank you.

To my family, particularly my mum and dad, who've always emphasized the importance of loving two things above all: Jesus, and a good meal! Dad, the original foodie, thank you for taking us everywhere from the shawarma joint around the corner, to the chili crab place in Singapore, all because you wanted to share that bite that you'd loved with us! We didn't just learn that food could break down barriers: we lived it, and that's thanks to you. Mum, thank you for sharing your never-ending enthusiasm for the art of cooking and hospitality, for answering every question about "that one curry" I've asked at wee hours of the night, for writing down every recipe in exacting detail. Thank you for your commitment to teaching us our roots through the dishes you cooked every day, no matter how tired you were after work. You are still my number one cooking inspiration. Thank you.

To my team: Jeffery Brooks, Harold Weitzberg, Nate Ernsberger, and the entire team at Redrock. When I met you, I was so thoroughly convinced that I didn't have anything to offer the world. Thank you for seeing that I did, for taking a risk on me, for always being in my corner.

To my recipe developers, Gerardo Cagigal and Morgan Hass: to have people at your level of expertise and talent validate these culinary bees in my bonnet takes my breath away! Thank you for your expert eye, for your ideas and amendments. But mostly, thank you for joining me in seeing these recipes as an act of service. Because of your care and excellence, I share these recipes with confidence. Thank you.

Thank you, Matt Armendariz, Adam Pearson, and Amy Paliwoda for making my recipes look like works of art, and for understanding what I meant when I said, "I want it to look like a cookbook in an old church."

Thank you, Sarah Sparks, Isla Vista Worship, Tekoa, Maverick Music, Jess Ray, Sandra McCracken, Citizens, Keith Green, Peter CottonTale, and the hundreds of other artists whose music carried me through every stage of this book.

Thank you to the entire team at DaySpring! This was a brand-new endeavor for you: a cookbook. Thank you for being willing to take a risk on me, for joining me in the belief this could be a gift to people who find the dinner hour to be more stressful than sacred. I have been so touched by the way you manage to be kind, but also committed to excellence. You are my people! Thank you specifically to my editor, Gini Wietecha. Your enthusiasm, sensitivity, and encouragement were so meaningful to me. Sometimes you're so caught up in something, you need a set of eyes on the outside telling you that you're on the right track. Thank you for being those eyes for

me. And thank you most especially for praying for me. I've never worked with an editor who prayed me through the process, and I don't think I can ever go without that again! Thank you!

And finally, I'd like to thank the Lord for inspiring me with this book idea even in the midst of my exasperation and disappointment. I was whining on the phone to my manager about yet another opportunity that had passed me by, and in my frustration I said, "I mean what am I supposed to do? Write a devotional cookbook or something?!"

Jeffery went quiet. And then murmured, "Well, that's a good idea."

Lord, even in the midst of my impatience and impertinence, You are faithful and kind to me. I can't comprehend it, really. But I can't wait to clink glasses and break bread with You, and You can explain it all to me. Thank You.

Amen.
Selah.

About the Author

AARTI SEQUEIRA is a cooking show host, cookbook author, journalist, television producer, and food personality. She is a mainstay on Food Network after winning season six of *Food Network Star* with her trademark combination of an infectious cackle and a unique signature food style: American favorites with an Indian soul. A passionate Christian, she also speaks to women of faith about overcoming fear and the sacred nature of breaking bread. She lives in North Carolina with her children and husband, actor Brendan McNamara. For more from Aarti, check out her collection at dayspring.com and several retails near you.

LIVE YOUR FAITH

Dear Friend,

This book was prayerfully crafted with you, the reader, in mind. Every word, every sentence, every page was thoughtfully written, designed, and packaged to encourage you—right where you are this very moment. At DaySpring, our vision is to see every person experience the life-changing message of God's love. So, as we worked through rough drafts, design changes, edits, and details, we prayed for you to deeply experience His unfailing love, indescribable peace, and pure joy. It is our sincere hope that through these Truth-filled pages your heart will be blessed, knowing that God cares about you—your desires and disappointments, your challenges and dreams.

He knows. He cares. He loves you unconditionally.

BLESSINGS!
THE DAYSPRING BOOK TEAM

———————

Additional copies of this book and
other DaySpring titles can be purchased
at fine retailers everywhere.
Order online at dayspring.com
or
by phone at 1-877-751-4347